THE COMPLETE GUIDE TO CREATIVE GIFT-GIVING

THE COMPLETE GUIDE TO CREATIVE GIFT-GIVING

Cynthia G. Yates

VB
VINE
BOOKS

SERVANT PUBLICATIONS
ANN ARBOR, MICHIGAN

Vine Books is an imprint of Servant Publications especially designed to
serve evangelical Christians.

Published by Servant Publications
P.O. Box 8617
Ann Arbor, Michigan 48107

97 98 99 00   10 9 8 7 6 5 4 3 2

Printed in the United States of America
ISBN 0-89283-997-X

LIBRARY OF CONGRESS CATALOGING-IN-PUBLICATION DATA

Yates, Cynthia
The complete guide to creative gift giving / Cynthia G. Yates.
    p.   cm.
ISBN 0-89283-997-X
1. Shopping.   2. Gifts.   3. Gift wraps.   I. Title.
TX335.Y295   1997
640'.73—dc21   97-14110
                                                 CIP

I dedicate this book to Jo Clayton,
who has taught me much about giving.

Contents

Acknowledgments

The usual "I want to thank my family and friends" applies to this book in a singular way. I *really* want to thank them—my family in particular—for sharing the gift of giving with me for so many years.

As you read this book, you will notice that the pages are filled with examples I have taken from my life experience. It took writing a book about giving to actually notice how giving a family I have! In particular, I want to acknowledge my mother and two sisters.

Special mention goes to the children who assisted with the kids' chapter:

A couple of outstanding nieces, Olivia and Leah Kahler.

Three terrific kids named Laura, Taylor, and Cameron Clayton.

Introduction

I do not own a glue gun. I probably should, but I had to return the one I bought. I couldn't figure out how it worked. Why do I tell you this? Because this is not a book about crafts, it is a book about creativity in gift-giving. The way I see it, there is a difference between creative people and crafty people. Creative people are always looking for interesting or different ways to do things. Crafty people are creative people with glue guns. (And the ability to use them!)

This is a book about using *your* creativity, with a little emphasis on the "path of least gift expenditure." My desire is to give you a gift of your own, a gift that will have long-lasting value, a gift that becomes dogeared and used. **This book is for you!** Park it next to your favorite cookbook or your phone directory. Turn to it often as you ponder the perfect present for your best friend, the third grade teacher, the mom-to-be, or your soul mate.

As complete as I've tried to make this, an *exhaustive* book on gift-giving would fill the Library of Congress and probably weigh as much as a '57 Pontiac! Why? Because there are as many gift ideas as there are *things*. Add personality, personal preference, talents, and interests—and the list is endless. *The*

Complete Guide to Creative Gift-Giving is written, therefore, to encourage you to *think* about personality, personal preference, and so on, when scouting the perfect gift for someone.

There are chapters in this book that zero in on specifics, such as the hard-to-buy-for, children, life's milestones, and holiday applications. But don't depend on just those chapters for ideas! The book is deliberately cluttered with clever concepts throughout. For instance, you may stumble across a perfect idea for Christmas in the chapter on presentation, or a stupendous scheme for your anniversary in the chapter on planning. If ever a book was meant to be underlined and highlighted, this is it! Write your own great ideas in the margins.

It was quite a challenge to keep the book filled with suggestions and not to repeat gift ideas from one chapter to the next. There *are* some repeated suggestions, however, which were special enough to be mentioned again (and again!). Some apply to several different situations. For example, planting a tree in someone's honor, an engraved Bible, and a terry cloth bathrobe make several appearances.

This is a fun book! It gives you answers and advice, as well as the incentive needed to become the most popular gift giver on the planet. It even gives you the gift of an occasional giggle. Enjoy!

1

The Gift of Giving
A SIGN OF OUR LOVE

Joseph Percival Yates was a cowboy. Born in England before the turn of the century, adventure summoned him across the Atlantic to the Sweet Grass Hills, smack on the border between Canada and Big Sky Country. The plucky little Englishman was one tough hombre who homesteaded those hills on a big red horse. Prohibition, the Depression, and World War II were only temporary roadblocks to his unfettered spirit. Then he met Dorothy. All of a sudden, cowboy, bootleg, and rascal days were over, and in the twilight of his life, he fathered a child. Utterly transformed with pride and delight in his small family, Joe settled into a blissful routine and doted on Dorothy. Theirs was a close and loving bond. Their evenings were spent touring the vast Montana prairie or listening to radio, curled together in an overstuffed chair, their child, little Joe, between them.

A county fair or a traveling salesman

never came to town without Joe's buying Dorothy a gift; a trip to the city was incomplete without a token of his love, dutifully wrapped and proudly presented. The same short note accompanied every single gift: "Devotedly, Joe." And so it went, Joe and Dorothy and baby.

One day Joe brought home an unusual gift for his by then five-year-old son. It was a dog named Belle. Belle was not just any dog. She was a full-grown Doberman pinscher, completely capable of giving her new master the kind of Doberman behavior one would expect. Belle would "watch and protect the child and Mama," said Joe. Two days after he brought the dog home, Joe was killed in a car accident.

As sorrowful a tale as this is, it is filled with meaning for me. Joseph Percival Yates, you see, would have been my father-in-law, and Joseph William Yates, the boy with the dog, is my husband.

Joe was young when his father died, but his father lived on in every gift he had given him. Belle fulfilled her role magnificently and became a constant companion to young Joe. She seemed to sense her special duty, and made her presence clear to every milkman, mailman, *and* stranger who approached the property.

Every single year, as I unpack our Christmas decorations, I think of Belle. Her name adorns a tree skirt that was given to Joe's mother, "Mama," as a gift: "Dorothy, Joe, and Belle," it reads. Thoughts of Belle bring me back to a plucky Englishman on a horse named Red, with wishful thoughts about what might have been. And when I make Christmas cookies in the old electric mixer that came home as a gift to Mama from a county fair, or when I dust a delicately carved wooden box that came with the predictable note, I think those thoughts some more. I remind myself that a gift can change in meaning and value suddenly, as suddenly as when an accident happens on the Montana prairie, when you are headed home to listen to radio with your small family.

∽

A Lasting Legacy

Look around you. Study the walls, the shelves, the furniture. Look at every lamp, book, picture, and knickknack. Think about the silverware in the kitchen drawer, the jewelry in the ballerina music box, the perfume on the dresser. Open your bedroom closet and have a glance, peek in the cupboards, look at the latest note of encouragement lying on your night stand. Chances are mighty good that some of the things you see came from others.

As I scan my small, rustic living room, I see several objects that came along with best wishes from friends and family. There is a silly old lariat on the wall from my sister Anne, an old-fashioned rocker from friends David and Tedi, a carved duck from a man we once befriended. Next to the lariat hangs a wooden sign that welcomes everyone "To The Lake," a birthday present from my sister Sheila. Leaning against a lamp is a handmade wooden frame surrounding a painting of woodland ferns, a gift from my neighbor, Leslie. These and other mementos crowd our living room, forever reminders of the place certain people have had in our lives, if only for a season. I cannot stop the broad smile that comes right now, with faraway thoughts that skip from face to face as I think of those who gave. Their gifts now share our living space as little memorials to friendship and love.

I wonder if many of us have thought of the lasting meaning and sentiment of the gifts we give. That piece of rope, wooden frame, and worn, leather rocker have found a place of permanence and significance in our lives.

Take a moment to consider all of the gifts you have given and received. Once you do, you will realize that gift-giving is a very big part of our lives, our traditions, and our emotions.

Giving gifts is a significant custom for all of mankind, and is woven throughout history. (One can only wonder how different it would be if the Magi brought aluminum foil, citronella, and lard to the Christ Child, instead of gold, frankincense, and myrrh, or if the French sent a lighthouse instead of the Statue of Liberty, or if Native Americans brought squirrel or possum to Thanksgiving dinner!)

If there is one sure thing, even throughout time, it is that gift-giving brings joy, lasting memory, and *challenge. Finding the right gift* can be daunting! Not anymore. Now that you have this book, you will face every holiday or special event with terrific ideas from which to choose, and over time, the book's margins can be filled with ideas of your own. From this day forward, the only hard part of gift-giving will be deciding which of these countless suggestions to consider!

❧

Happy Birthday, Mather

"To a verey speichle prosne, Mom!" was written on a pink card so many, many years ago. Inside was a tender note: "When I think of you a spechle feeling come in to my leef, Love, Josh." The card accompanied a piece of wood onto which he'd glued alphabet noodles. It said, "The Lord is my shep." I still have that card and cherish that piece of wood. Yes, the Lord is my shep—and Josh still can't spel.

❧

Why Do We Give?

We give gifts to honor others, whether for personal accomplishment, life passage, or simply because of feelings of friendship and love. Our gifts bear tidings of goodwill, of kindness, of praise, or respect. We give because we *want* to give.

Not all giving bears a price tag or comes in a gaily decorated package. A glance at our daily lives will testify to the constant flow of gifts between friends: a welcome handshake, an extra effort to please someone, a word of endearment (to a verey speichle prosne!), a gentle reminder of unconditional love. Every smile, touch, or hug is part of our human expression, and brings a message of tenderness and a feeling of well-being.

We, ourselves, can be a precious gift to others. Offering our support, listening to a wounded heart, or being present during a time of need are all examples of our gift of self.

Just as you looked around your home and saw the legacy of friends through their gifts to you, watch for the special touch of others on your life today. And be ever aware of possibilities to give these unwrapped, cost-free gifts to those around you. Let me share a tender story that shows the power of the gift of love in yet another way. It is a true story about a single mom.

∿

Love Came to Kathy

Kathy had made wrong choices in life. That fact, coupled with recent circumstances, left her in a messy predicament. She was temporarily homeless, broke, stranded in an unfamiliar and remote area, and solely responsible for her young son. To make matters worse, it was Christmas Eve. Things did not look good for Kathy, as she fought wave after wave of despair and panic with feeble determination to survive. Thoughts of tomorrow were too much to bear, for today was soon enough for the sorrow that covered her heart with darkness.

Learning of her dilemma, a country priest found a cabin for Kathy and her boy, and settled them in. The chaos of her moment, though, kept Kathy from sharing how desperate her situation really was. An inventory of her possessions that day included a blanket, two toothbrushes, an old rattletrap Ford van, and a can of tuna. There wasn't even a can opener in sight. No one knew the depth of her trouble but Kathy herself—and the One who knows all. Little did Kathy know during that hopeless episode that Almighty God was looking with love and favor on her and her child. He was seeing her with the same love and favor he had sent down once before on a long-ago Christmas Eve.

From outside her cabin came the sure sound of tires

crunching cold, dry snow. People—strangers—came to Kathy's door with an invitation to dinner. They scooped up mother and child and took them to a home crammed with warmth and cheer. Kathy and her boy were nourished in body and spirit. They were loved without judgment or scorn. They were welcomed as friends.

The car's headlights gave them a glimpse of the little cabin in the snow as the priest drove Kathy and her son to their new home once again. Armed with a plate of cookies and guiding her little boy to the door, she smiled broadly and waved good-bye. Yes, they'd come to Christmas service in the morning if someone came to get them. Tires crunched snow once more as the kindly man drove off, and Kathy stepped inside. She gasped. Her little boy stood in wonder. Someone had been in her cabin. In the corner of the sparse room stood a small fir tree, ablaze with festive lights. A few homemade ornaments poked out from beneath an avalanche of artificial icicles. And under the tree were two presents.

The lights blazing on that tree brought hope and banished anxious thoughts about tomorrow. Fearful tomorrows were gone for good because of the gift of love from strangers. Love came to Kathy that Christmas Eve, perfected through the gift of giving.

∽

Kindness, compassion, unconditional love, and selfless sharing do not need big red bows or Christmas tree tinsel. They are gifts of immeasurable value. We must remember the importance of sharing these qualities with friends and strangers alike.

A Sign of Our Love

There is no denying, though, that we are motivated by our feelings to want to give a *token* of love and friendship to others. Presenting the perfect gift brings us a moment of unsurpassable joy, as the old adage "It is better to give than to receive" rings with certainty in our hearts. What a thrill to watch as elderly fingers work to unwrap pretty ribbon, or as a saucer-eyed little girl squeals and jumps in anticipation of her present. We are always eager to give just the right gift that says, "Hey, I thought about you!"

It *Is* the Thought That Counts!

Did you know that cost is not the main factor in the gifts we give? Intent, effort, and meaning are the factors that matter, and come through loud and clear when we give a gift. For instance, a friend of limited means recently gave us a simple present (a piece of wood that looks great in our home), and clearly took care crafting the tissue paper wrapping, and topping it off with dried wild flowers. Our friendship was honored by this simple, yet conspicuous effort.

With an eye toward using your creative genius, determination to honor the recipient with a bit of your own enterprise, and the help of this book, gift-giving will become what it is meant to be: an expression of love or appreciation that is truly given, truly received, and truly felt.

When Do We Give?

Hoo, boy! When you add up the "whens," you face the "whys?" with renewed resolve! It was only after we established a budget in our household that we realized how much of our money went to the benefit of others! *Gift-giving is an expensive, year-long proposition.* Precisely because of this, it must be regarded with sensible planning. Just as it is poor stewardship to career down the grocery aisle pitching every whim and fancy into our carts, so is it foolish to wait until a gift is needed and then shop.

If we wait for every birthday, anniversary, housewarming, dinner party, wedding, engagement, baby shower, new baby, condolence call, graduation, celebration, just-because, illness, my-friend-needs-a-pick-me-up, thank you, romantic notion, as well as Christmas, Chanukah, Valentine's Day, Thanksgiving, Mother/Father/Grandparents' Day, Easter (whew) to roll around for every mate, parent, child, niece, nephew, in-law, pastor, grandparent, friend, friend's children (are you still with me?)—then we are likely to face gift-giving with drudgery and despair. But not anymore, because this book will guide you to a systematic approach to giving. Chapter Two, in particular, will encourage you to establish a *plan*. For instance, is there a wedding in the future? A baby shower? A graduation? A milestone birthday? (Last year we faced my mother's eightieth and our son's twenty-fifth—times for special celebration.) Once you have "sketched" the year, you will be able to determine a specific dollar amount for your gift budget. You might also be able to determine that you need *smelling salts*—a great gag gift, by the way, for the father of the bride!

Writing everything down is a good thing to do, because it gives you a chance to look at your obligations reasonably and realistically. It might also compel you to reconsider your choice of gift or become creative about its purchase. Your list could not possibly include spontaneous gifts (especially in the romance department), but that's OK ... this book has enough ideas to cover those unplanned gift obligations. Dig into its pages for more ideas than you'll ever be able to use.

Hint, Hint, Hint

Three helpful hints are important to set you on the path of "least gift expenditure" and to aid in your search for the perfect gift:

1. *Keep Your Eyes and Ears Open*

I like to think I'm a genius of creativity and that all of my ideas come naturally, but truthfully that is not the case. What I am is *observant*. For example, I am always studying catalogues, store displays, the latest products, and the way other people decorate their homes or yards. If I like something and think it is possible to duplicate—usually with my own twist—I will store the idea in my brain. Almost always, I am able to find a more creative (less expensive) way to accomplish my goal. One perfect illustration of this principle in action is my use of baskets to consolidate several items into one gift. Catalogues routinely offer gift baskets. Study the ads and fill your basket with delight!

Being alert has also helped me with price comparisons and with recognizing a good sale. If I encounter a spectacular purchase on a gift-worthy item, I will often add it to my gift "stash," sometimes with no particular recipient in mind. Most recently, I came across a closeout rack of brushed-suede women's vests. The price was so unbelievably low, I questioned the clerk for fear I'd get caught stealing! By the time you read this, three of those vests will have made an appearance under our Christmas tree.

2. *Roll Up Your Sleeves*

Homemade ranks high with me! I did not, however, want to write a book on crafts, but on the art and act of gift-giving. There are books on *crafts* galore—my intent was to write a book with *ideas* galore. One reason why is that many of us do not have the facility, the equipment, or the time to make something from scratch. (Other chapters in this book give attention to gifts from the kitchen—something most of us *can* manage from scratch.)

But there is no denying—if you are looking for the path of least expenditure, this is usually the way to go. If you take the first principle to keep your eyes and ears open, and apply it to "make it yourself," you can come up with dandy ideas. Two of my latest gifts came from such inspiration:

- A neighbor has a six-foot-long "mobile," made of short, weathered pieces of driftwood hanging next to her front door. This adds a charming look. I could do that! I scoured our beach for short chunks of driftwood, bored a small hole smack through the middle of each piece, and ran heavy wire down the middle. Awesome gift! Made one for myself.

- An elderly friend wanted a hanging basket for *her* entranceway. By purchasing a few plants, a planter, some potting soil, and crisscrossing heavy twine underneath, I presented her with a flower arrangement to be proud of— at less than half the cost of one purchased from a nursery.

3. *Shop Year-Round*

Learn to shop year-round and stash gifts away. Let me tell you what I mean: For so long that it has become a tradition, my husband and I waltz into a specialty shop in our small town on the very first business day after Christmas to buy next year's ornaments! Our family presents a new ornament to one another every single Christmas—some years this is our only gift, by choice. We have always given our son, Josh, a high-quality ornament, in anticipation of the time he would be off celebrating Christmas on his own. The store owner greets us and knows why we are there: 50 percent off. After purchase, ornaments are boxed, marked, and stored in the brown store sack on the top shelf of our closet. It is a treat to pull the sack down, blow off the dust, and explore last year's purchase when Christmas rolls around again.

You can save a lot of money shopping for things off-season. Clothing stores offer slashed prices on winter clothes beginning sometime in February, on summer clothes around August. Look for clearance racks, usually toward the back of the store. Buy a good-quality sweater for your husband or wife for up to 75 percent off, an infant snowsuit for the mom-to-be, a lacy blouse for a cousin's birthday. Do the same thing with children's toys. If you run across a closeout and can purchase several of the same item, you are set for a number of children's birthday parties!

Find a spot in your home where you can stash gifts as you buy them. Try to buy with purpose. When the rest of the world marches to the beat of the *frantic find* in December you can sit back, sip eggnog, and laugh.

2

Give Without Going Broke
OUT WITH WILLY-NILLY GIFT-GIVING

It's December. You pour a cup of hot chocolate, open a brand new notebook, and begin your list: husband or wife, kids, parents, grandparents, a bazillion relatives, bosses, neighbors, friends, the list goes on, extending into the next page with names in a neat, long column. Grandma Alex—what do you get someone who is eighty? Uncle Rick—what do you get for a guy who has everything? Loren—how do you repay the trustworthy mechanic who saved you bundles in car repair?

It's May. You stare at the mile-high pile of wedding and graduation announcements that seems to double in size daily as if it were cloning itself while you sleep. Your kids have grown—and so have their friends. Teenagers who used to forage to exhaustion in your refrigerator are now inviting you to share in their passage to young adulthood. It's not all pomp and circumstance for *you* as your eyes bulge right along with the growing pile of invitations.

It's a week before your wedding anniversary—and you remembered! You are so proud (and relieved) to be on top of it this year, you wish you could move the date up a few days, just to prove that *you remembered first!* So what do you do? Flowers and dinner are standard fare, but you want to do something *special*. And just where *is* the tag on her nightgown that tells you her size, anyway?

∾

Sound familiar? It should. Sooner or later, just about everybody faces the dilemma of *have to get*, *what to get*, and *how to afford*. For some, the answer is easy: a tradition has been in place (we celebrate our anniversary at the charming inn where our wedding reception was held), or they give a "collection" gift each year (remember our Christmas ornaments?). That kind of gift has lasting merit and is as much fun in anticipation as in participation. Yet there are gift occasions that test your mettle: you really, *really*, want to do something different this time. If you feel as if your brain is in neutral when it comes to creativity, or that you'd have to rob a stagecoach to pay for all your gifts, take heart! You can easily be creative and frugal, *and* beam with pride as you present a unique gift to a special person. This book will see to that!

Frugal Does Not Mean Cheap

There is a particular message I wish to convey right now. It is from the credo of my first book, *1001 Bright Ideas to Stretch Your Dollars*, and it is this: "I don't want to be a tightwad. I want to be frugal. I want to celebrate life." Do you? At times I worry that our concern over budgets, deficits, Dow Jones averages, and double-coupon days at the market has made tightfisted grumps of us all. Humbug! We *can* live within our means without drudgery. Frugal, you see, does not equate with penny-pinching Scrooginess. It equates with SMART! And even though this book is not about frugal living, it incorporates philosophies and concepts that spring from smart financial finagling.

So, where do you begin? You begin with a plan.

The Plan

Every business needs a plan, and in this business of gift-giving, you need one too! Assemble that notepad, a calendar, your address book, or put your list of people who share your life experience on computer. Begin with your calendar: write a list of every single occasion you can think of for the coming year. Include birthdays, important anniversaries, holidays, any upcoming events, such as graduations, engagements, weddings, babies, confirmations, Bar/Bat Mitzvahs, "milestone" events in someone's life such as retirement, first book published, *anything* you can conjure up that might require some sort of gift.

Next to each event, immediately write the names of everyone to whom you might give a gift. Christmas will probably lead the parade with several names; your own anniversary would simply have the name of your mate. Go through your address book. Think hard. If your children are grown, is there a cluster of young adults who are their friends? Do you anticipate wedding, graduation, or birth announcements from them? Think about your neighborhood. Do you usually share gifts with neighbors? What about the elderly man down the street who would probably appreciate a no-cost gift of laughter and good conversation (or good listening!)? Think about the people at work. Think about the people at the store, the gas station, the post office. Think about the UPS driver, the pet groomer, the doctor, the dentist.

Certainly not everyone you think of will be on your list. As a matter of fact, it is a good idea to make a first list, and then a second, and a third. Maybe the first could be a true "Wish List" with mention of everyone to whom you'd *like* to give a gift. Some of *those* people might only get a gaily decorated popcorn ball and a card! Some may get a phone call, some nothing at all. You are writing your plan in ink, not blood.

As a matter of fact, unless you are a whiz with that glue gun and can whip up easy and cost-free presents, expect to shrink your list to fit your intentions *and* your wallet. A sample list:

CHRISTMAS		
NAME	GIFT IDEA	BUDGET

Holidays

Not everyone gives gifts for all of these holidays, but here is a sampling of the dates most likely to present you with gift-giving opportunities:

- New Year's Day: January 1 (or as my friend Matthew would say, January the 1th)
- Valentine's Day: February 14
- Easter: dependent on calendar
- Mother's Day: second Sunday in May (normally)
- Father's Day: second Sunday in June (normally)
- Grandparents' Day: second Sunday in September (normally)
- Secretary's Day: end of April
- Thanksgiving Day: last Thursday in November
- Chanukah: dependent on calendar
- Christmas: December 25
- Kwanzaa (Swahili for "first fruits," celebrated by African-Americans): seven days beginning December 26

Special Days

- Birthday
- Anniversary
- Graduation
- Retirement
- Wedding
- Childbirth/Adoption
- Baptism/Christening
- Bar/Bat Mitzvah
- Confirmation

Pre-Planning

It takes work to make a list and to pre-plan, and not all gifts can or will be purchased in advance. One thing can't be denied: Pre-planning will help lighten your load, and you'll be able to take advantage of sales.

Study your gift list with the discipline of a Rhodes scholar. Suppose you have to give three new baby presents during the next six months? Call local stores and ask when seasonal sales are expected. There are at least two times each year when stores close out merchandise: end of summer and end of winter. There is also a baby week when items for infants go on sale. With good planning, you could buy three toddler snowsuits for as much as 75 percent off. It may seem silly to present a July baby with a snowsuit, but I guarantee it will be appreciated by Mama when that first cold blast of winter hits. Baby expected in the winter? Present a beach outfit, complete with sand pail and shovel. *Always* browse closeouts and sales with an eye toward gifting. For instance, I was in a national discount store one day and saw a sign: "Easter merchandise 90 percent off." I marched to the shelves to find an excellent assortment of baskets, some for as little as nineteen cents! I bought a few and cut off the "Easter" handles, which were too seasonal for my purpose. These baskets became containers for future gifts of bread or cookies.

Are you a wizard in the kitchen? Give food or baked goods. Holidays, funerals, and in some cases birthdays, are great opportunities to let your culinary talents shine. A batch of brownies at a bridal shower might not go over well. *Unless*, of course, they are presented with the necessary recipe, ingredients, and pan for baking them.

Write down any specific ideas you have for people on your list right now. Do you know for certain you are going to give money to the newlyweds? Write it down. Are you sure you will give a savings bond to your godson? Write it down. Do you always give your best friend a cookbook? Whatever the gift, write it down with the projected cost. Evaluate your list at the beginning of each month; try to look a few months ahead. You need not always be shopping for gifts, but you should have an idea for a gift tucked in the back of your brain someplace.

Just the other day I visited "my" thrift store. This was a true visit to chat with the manager; I had no intention of spending money. Yet there was a brand new pair of white cotton shorts from a fancy uptown shop. The price tag was still attached! The shorts came with a leather belt and would be perfect for my mother. I paid three dollars and toted them home. Why? Mother's Day was one month away. Let me tell you, she looks dynamite in those shorts and couldn't care less if I paid three dollars or thirty dollars.

Gifts need not be purchased with specific intent. I use the top shelf in my closet to stash items that will be considered at some future date when I need a present. Some items that are on the shelf right now: a "Noah's Ark" wallpaper border, a designer sweatshirt, a high-quality cookbook given to me during a department store giveaway, a few mugs, a wall hanging that is not suitable for our home, several books bought at dirt-cheap prices during closeouts. Think of the possibilities!

Now it is your turn to look for possibilities. Find a spot in your home where you can safely stash items that are gift-worthy. Wander through your home and look. I bet you not only find the perfect place, but that you also come up with a few items to "seed" that spot right now!

The Budget

If you made any kind of list, most likely you have recognized—maybe for the first time—what a big chunk of moola this business of gift-giving requires! This is an area that is often overlooked when people budget finances. Once again, *gift-giving is an expensive proposition.* For precisely that reason, this book presents some alternatives to costly gifts and encourages you to think ahead so that you can buy ahead. For instance, with (count them) *thirteen* weddings this year, I am going to take advantage of the annual spring white sale offered by a national store. Or I might purchase high-quality books suitable for a newly married couple if I can find some offered through a discount book catalogue. I may also roll up my sleeves and with the help of my computer and printer, fill a sturdy wooden recipe box with favorite recipes and cooking tips.

If you continue to buy gifts at the time the need presents itself, you will most certainly spend more money than necessary and most *likely* end up with just what you set out to get: a last-minute gift. I recommend that you establish a monthly "gift budget" and do your best to creatively spend way below the projected amount. Try to project dollar amounts right now, and don't write it in ink! Use a pencil with a fat eraser. Keep in mind that this is your *projected* list. It doesn't take into account sudden developments or romantic whims.

❧

A Special Doll

"So what's the neatest gift you ever received?" I yelled above the whir of the blow-dryer. Beth ran the brush through my hair a little more deliberately as she thought. "It was from my dad," she said. "It was a doll."

"Why was it so special?" I brought my voice down to normal range as she switched off the dryer. My question clearly jogged Beth's memory banks and evoked a feeling of warmth and sentiment that settled on the room.

Beth told me the doll was special because she knew her father *actually* picked it out for her. "Usually we kids would open presents and say 'Thanks, Mom and Dad,' and we could tell that our father had no idea what was in the box. This time I knew he'd bought it himself."

Beth turned on the dryer and went back to work on my hair. I thought about what she said. I remembered a red sweater my father picked out for me when I was young. I remembered that it was particularly special to me, too, because he did it on his own.

If the Shoe Fits, She'll Wear It

OK, Romeo. Now that you have your anniversary down to a fine science, what are you going to get for your wife? You don't want to run around the mall on your lunch hour without any forethought, do you? Of course not! You want to present something that shows how on the ball you've been this year ... you want the love of your life to get the message that you put your all into this. What do you get? And how do you know what size? Or color? Or style? Or fabric?

Many years ago my husband came home with a big, gaily decorated box. It was a present for me. He knew I wished for a long sundress, a casual and stylish smock I could wear when gallivanting around town. (I must have seen something in a catalogue.) The charm of Joseph actually buying something like this was preempted by my excitement! I envisioned myself waltzing around the local farmers market, basket in hand, wearing my new dress. How miserable I felt when I opened the box! It was a Swiss dot, empire waist, two sizes too small, *young teen* prom dress! If I showed up anyplace in that outfit I'd be a candidate for "Unsolved Mysteries"! It would be about the same as me giving him a Nehru jacket and white patent leather loafers. I didn't hide my crushing disappointment. It took years before Joe got the nerve to buy me anything besides candy and perfume.

Guidelines to Help With Your Gift Quest

- **Age.** Do NOT give Grandma roller skates for her birthday! Think about the age and the physical condition of the person before you impulsively buy. For instance, just as young people groan at the practical presents of Christmas (to them, such a waste of perfectly good money!), older folk seldom have use for unnecessary clutter. I have several mature friends who are, quite simply, doodadded out! And they hate to dust all those cutesy little knickknacks. Try to be sensible when considering age constraints. And give the kids a toy!

- **Gender.** No matter how politically correct the world tries to make us, the bottom line is that men like things that have working parts. It's a genetic thing. Give my husband a *thing* that he can take apart and put together again—or a tool—

and he is in seventh heaven. Give him a tie and expect a polite yawn. Women like *things,* too. Especially when they have long green stems and fit in a vase.

- **Occupation.** What does/did the person do for a living? Can you find a gift that fits the job? My sister recently gave me a plastic copy holder to hold my papers when I am typing. You could give a budding architect a book on architecture, a forester a new compass, a truck driver the audio tape of a new bestseller. How about a nifty lunch kit for the new brown-bagger in the family?

- **Hobbies.** If the person has a hobby, gift-giving is a snap! Hobbyists are thrilled with anything that adds to their projects. How about a caboose for the friend who collects miniature trains? Or salt and pepper shakers for your aunt whose walls are lined with the strangest sets you ever did see? Or an old Coke bottle you picked up for a song at a garage sale for the friend with the "country kitchen"?

- **Interests.** A book on philosophy would rate a hearty "Yahoo!" when I peel off the paper. A best-selling romance? About as much excitement for me as watching paint dry. Bring me an exotic new herb or spice to use for dinner and I'll follow you anywhere. A cookbook using lots of artificial ingredients? Sorry. *Everyone* has particular interests. Those interests might not be interesting to you, but keep them in mind when wondering what to get. Do you have a quiet friend who spends time fishing? Drop by a sporting goods store and have a chat with one of the clerks for gift ideas. Someday you might just hear a faint "Yahoo!" coming from the old mill stream!

- **Religious inclinations.** Separate from spiritual passages such as child or adult baptisms, first communions, and Bar Mitzvahs, which often require a gift, there are those who tend toward the spiritual and always welcome anything that reminds them of their faith. Daily "flip" calendars which come in the form of devotionals or meditations are quite popular, most especially among the elderly. Lovely photos and pictures are sold at religious bookstores, as are cards that express deepest sentiments of faith. These stores usually have a fun assortment of children's Bibles and storybooks. The music departments of many stores offer tapes of favorite hymns or the latest popular group among teens.
- **Sports.** Here is another easy category. Does your daughter-in-law play tennis? Consider socks, balls, visor, wristbands, lessons, and racquets as potential gifts. Suppose your son likes to ride his bike over hill and dale? There are endless gadgets and clothes designed for the new breed of bike riders. Does your niece have a pony? Visit the farm and ranch store and buy a lead rope or a fancy new halter.
- **Favorite color.** There are two ways of looking at color: what someone *likes* best and what *looks* best on someone. For instance, give my husband anything beige and he becomes the invisible man. Put red on me and you can see me coming from as far away as New Jersey! What is the person's favorite color? (If he disappears in beige, throw in a colorful tie!) Is there a color scheme in that person's house? Would maroon dish towels look out of place? Would wild splashes of color on placemats be out of the question?
- **Personality.** A boldly patterned tie might not be the smartest thing to give Uncle Frank with the dour outlook on

life. Personality plays a role when determining what to give. Is the person extroverted? Get something flashy and on the cutting edge of fun or daring. Introverted? Try a nice, quiet book.

- **Motor skill:** Don't get an intricate puzzle for the in-law who can't chew gum and walk at the same time! When considering a toy or a gadget, think of physical capabilities.

- **Size:** I am *forever* returning "medium" for "large." (Most people are astonished to learn I weigh about as much as our stove!) This is not only embarrassing, it is a nuisance. So how do you size up size without getting yourself in extra-large trouble? Ask, if possible. If not, try to get a peek at a label on the jacket or coat. Or, sneak into the bedroom and read labels of clothes in the closet. HUSBANDS, BEWARE! Every woman alive has clothes in her closet for when she "loses that extra ten pounds." If you check a garment, make sure it is something she wears regularly. Clerks in clothing stores are helpful if you can generalize about body size. And I have commandeered more than one barrel-chested man in a store to try something on before I toted it home to my Joe.

- **Outdoorsy or indoorsy.** I love the outdoors, and I'm a permanent fixture next to our campfire (we live on a lake) in the summer. But I hibernate in winter. I hate to be outside when it is cold. A ski pass or a pair of skates would probably not be a wise choice for me: mufflers and mittens would! Picnic gear, on the other hand, would score a big hit. Does your friend putter around outside or walk every day? Buy an interesting bulb collection, a potted plant, a bird feeder, a book about wildflowers. If the person prefers the indoors, maybe a silk plant and a video about birds would make more sense.

- **Musical interests.** Music is such balm for our souls. It soothes, it lulls, it energizes, it motivates. Music can get your toes to tapping. Does your friend tap to the beat of steel drums, bagpipes, Celtic songs, the latest jazz group or rock band? Buy a tape or CD or tickets to a concert. Does your friend sing or play an instrument? Go to a music store! Buy sheet music!

A Word About Receiving Gifts

This entire book is about giving. You probably invested in this book because you do believe it's more blessed to give than to receive. There is much to say about that. I've read many times, for instance, that *love* isn't even real until it is given away. One of the most touching comments Joseph ever made was that I doubled his joy by being an eager recipient of his love and attention.

But this is worth mention: some of us may need grace to accept gifts that are given freely by others, because, for some, not only is it more "blessed to give," frankly, it's downright *easier.* Receiving a gift is as hard as receiving a compliment for some folks. If you fit that description, try to honor the person who has given you a gift with grace—and thanks.

Inappropriate Gifts

Two things are certain: you *will* give an inappropriate gift and you *will* receive an inappropriate gift. Please don't be insensitive about this! Some of the most meaningful presents we've received head the list in the "least likely for us to pick" department, but come with such sentiment and intent, they sit in a place of honor in our home. There are times, however, when you are given something that is unsuitable for a myriad of reasons: size, color, style … and personal beliefs. When that happens there are still two certain things to express: grace and thanks.

I am reminded of a father of two young children. This man made a rule for his home: there would be none of the computer or VCR-driven "games" that are popular today. Last Christmas his son opened a gift to find a Nintendo from a well-meaning relative. The child immediately looked at his dad, who was kind, but firm: "Do not disturb the wrapping, the game will be returned to the store." Good to his word, the father and son went to return the expensive toy. The boy was completely surprised when the clerk was instructed to hand him the refund. It was the boy's to spend wisely, said the dad. The young lad purchased an expensive "all-in-one" pocket tool that came in a leather case to attach to his belt. That child was on our beach yesterday. He used his tool to carve a point on a big stick and found a feather to stick in the top. Then he and the dogs wandered up and down the shore doing the stuff of little boys and dogs. Far better than sitting in front of a TV!

3

Why Didn't I Think of That!

THE KINDS OF GIFTS WE GIVE

There is more to gift-giving than meets the eye! Much more than fancy wrapping paper and curly ribbon, as an expression of love, friendship, gratitude, or sympathy, gift-giving is a matter of heart.

We've all picked out our share of "token" gifts, slapped down our shekels, paid the store to wrap them, and that was that. Sometimes it was the easiest thing to do. But if you've slapped down some of your shekels for this book, you are interested in more than perfunctory gifts: you want to maximize your "present potential" and maybe *save* some shekels in the process! Welcome to *Gifts 101*, a crash course in different *kinds* of gifts. The clear intent of this chapter is to get you thinking. My hope is to present concepts, aided by specific applications, and let *your* creative genius do the rest! We will explore giving from as broad a perspective as we can, and look at options beyond the "run-to-the-store-and-plop-your-money-down-without-much-thought" variety.

There are clear distinctions among the types of gifts we give. Come along with me now, as we explore different concepts in gift-giving and begin to look at examples of each. These options include no-cost, low-cost, food, spiritual, romantic, keepsake, gift certificates, sentimental collections, and the "group" gift.

No Cost

Know what? No-cost gifts can be the most expensive of all. It's true, because this category includes gifts that involve personal sacrifice, time, and effort. It is much easier to deliver a present than to offer help or service to someone. Others recognize the value of your sacrifice as more and more gifts bring the promise of time and effort. Some suggestions follow:

Time

- A popular gift for parents is baby-sitting. This is no small gesture. Finding (and affording) a trustworthy and competent baby-sitter for children is becoming difficult. Give a tired mom an afternoon off, or send a couple out for a romantic evening. Or do what we did for our pastor and his wife: trade houses for the night. Tell them to leave the kids with you. Send the couple to your house where dinner is waiting, soft music is playing, and the phone isn't ringing. Make sure you tell them to leave the dishes in the sink. *Alert: don't merely present a "certificate" for free baby-sitting. Parents say they are reluctant to burden the donor. Try to be specific about your offer.

- "Baby-sitting" does not always apply to children. Do you know someone who is tied to home or farm because of responsibility to animals? An offer to care for the critters for a weekend might be received with enthusiasm. There is another aspect to this that needs mention. The value of *this* gift is priceless: your offer to relieve the caregiver of a disabled or ill person. It is a gift without measure. This was done for us. When Mama came to our home to die, she had to be cared for around the clock. Friends sat with her so Joe and I could attend our son's football game, tend to business, or walk the beach and weep. In a sense, we gave Mama a gift she wanted very much. She died in our bedroom as she wished. We are thankful for others who helped us along the way.

Effort

Remember! This is *Gifts 101* and my purpose is to get *your* creative juices percolating! The ideas for no-cost gifts in *this* department are endless.

- Is there a car owner alive who wouldn't gladly thrust his keys into your hand if you offered to wash and clean the car? I would gladly hand over two sets right now … no questions asked!

- Would your best friend think of you every time she looked through her recently washed kitchen window? We did this for a friend who was ill. She returned from the hospital to squeaky clean windows.

- Know what happened when my husband broke his back last summer? A young friend hauled her dad over here and our lawn was trimmed to within an inch of its life! We were speechless.

- Do you have friends who need a pick-me-up? Drive over and announce you're the cook. When they ask what you're making, tell them it's the "blue plate special." It doesn't matter what it is. Make tuna on toast if you have to. Then, play cards afterward.

- Do you fish, camp, hike? Could you take someone with you?

Get the point? Can you defrost a freezer and inventory the contents for someone? Can you clean house, iron, weed a garden, wash and style a friend's hair? Think of something you'd like done for yourself. Then move the shoe to the other foot and do it for another!

Good Intentions Sometimes Land Us in Trouble

Styling someone's hair is one gift anyone who knows me would beg NOT to receive! I once used electric clippers on our son—Santa Monica Freeway right down the back of his head! People run screaming when I walk into a room with comb and scissors. I even created a new breed when I tried to clip our spaniel. All of this is to warn you to think twice before you barge into someone's life with good intentions.

Personal

Nearly everyone has a project or plan collecting dust. Maybe you could creatively use that project as a gift idea.

- One young woman was downright frustrated about her friend. "She has everything already!" she lamented. One day during coffee the has-everything friend dumped a pile of tattered papers on her table and searched for a recipe. Guess what she got for Christmas? A tidy recipe box filled with glued, taped, and rewritten recipes ... in alphabetical order!
- Could you do the same with photos? Or with a file folder filled with newspaper articles? I'd be thrilled if someone just did my *filing*!

Things

How do you come up with a *thing* that doesn't cost money?
Easy.

- My niece recently gave my sister a hefty river rock for her landscaping project. The young girl scoured river banks until she found the "right" rock.
- I've given two "matching" rocks to be used as bookends. Wish now I had them myself.
- Creation offers lots of ideas: branches, boughs, tall grass, golden wheat, a fistful of wildflowers.
- My neighbor (who owns a glue gun) uses bark, branches, and driftwood to create remarkable centerpieces and wreaths, or to decorate wooden picture frames.
- Do you have a houseplant? One friend gave me an ivy clipping from a Presbyterian church in Pennsylvania. I think of that dear woman every time I water my "Presbyterian ivy."
- I once gave my mom my entire year's collection of a cooking magazine.
- A friend just received a year's supply of a timeless magazine her daughter got for free from the library.

"Look Around You, Again"

A favorite gift idea is to give something we own that someone has admired. The joy of receiving will be doubled as the person recognizes your sacrifice. (I can tell you from firsthand experience that the joy of *giving* is quadrupled!)

*A word of caution: this can get out of hand. It is uncomfortable to visit someone who gives everything away just because it was admired.

The Best Gift of All

How about edification, affirmation, and acknowledgment? Wouldn't it be neat if you pasted a note on the fridge or on the bathroom mirror that acknowledged something about a family member or friend?

Low Cost

Remember my claim that cost is not the main factor in gift-giving, but effort and care? I'm going to prove that with some rope, a torn piece of a grocery bag, and an old, leather boot lace.

For his birthday last year, my sister gave Joe a six-dollar *used* lariat she found in a bin at the feed store. (A *used lariat bin?!*) We do not have horses, we are not cowboys, but we like Western stuff. The lariat was wound like a wreath. Anne ripped a piece of the bag into a boot shape and tied it to the rope with a shoelace from a hiking boot. (Anne does not own a glue gun, either.) This is what she wrote on the paper: "This here belongd to Wild Bill when he mosied thru Montana lookin fer baer. It's a mite bit short cause its been nawed on by grizzlies. But it still works real gud!"

That rope hangs prominently on our wall and is one of the most commented-upon objects in our home.

Find Your Creative Genius

You are creative. You might just have to look for your *level* of creativity. Incentive comes from some inside place, but once you decide to use your imagination, skill will come. And you will probably amaze yourself. I tell you this because creativity is a vital component to finding *and* presenting low-cost gifts.

There are literally thousands of gifts for under ten dollars if you know where and how to look. For now, let me mention two things: thrift stores and the person's interests.

Thrift Stores, Etc.

The "etc." stands for yard sales, garage sales, rummage sales, bazaars, pennysaver ads, consignment shops, junk stores, and second-hand stores. I do not include pawn shops, because I personally refuse to profit from someone's loss. A pawn shop might be a perfectly fine choice for you.

What do you look for in a place like this? I mean, do you SHOP for *presents* in a thrift store? Well, not exactly. Let me tell you what I do:

I rarely (as in, practically never) go to yard sales. I go to one local thrift shop which is run on behalf of developmentally disabled people, who also work at the store. I go to "my" store routinely, and follow a routine when I am there. I begin on one wall and scan housewares, then scout the edges, then the middle, followed by a thorough investigation of clothing racks. What do I look for? Absolutely nothing; I often leave empty-handed. Yet as I survey my little store, I am ever on alert for something to catch my eye. For instance:

• *Anything* that meets three criteria—old, green, and kitchen—is instantly scooped up for a friend. I recently found a turn-of-the-century meat fork with peeling green paint on the handle, which my friend would love. Nineteen cents. I used it to "adorn" a box that carried her Christmas present: a squat, green ceramic pitcher with raised flowers on the side. Four dollars. The pitcher was filled with Belgian chocolate and rested on a sea of popcorn balls.

- I look closely at books on display. I am not looking for *a* book, just looking. I once found a brand new current edition of a Richard Foster book on prayer. A call to a book store gave me the cost: $17.99. I paid seventy-nine cents, and a friend who likes Richard Foster will be dizzy with delight.

- When I scrutinize clothes I look for quality. I check labels, inspect fabric, condition, size, color. I might hit a mother lode at the men's rack if someone just cleaned her husband's closet—many of the clothes in these shops have never been worn.

And so I just look. Every now and then something catches my eye and I buy. Then I hug my friends and head home grinning.

Person's Interest

Can you find a gift that suits a person's interests? Does the person read particular books or enjoy a sport or hobby? Is the person spiritual? musical? artistic? outdoorsy? What kind of store does that person spend serious time in? Spend some serious time there yourself. Bring pad and paper. Study the inventory. Tell the clerk what you're doing—you might end up with an assistant! Dig into your creative genius and get inspired. Let me help you along.

Everyone knows I am a happy cook. Put me in a kitchen gadget shop and I am lost to the world. I visited one of these shops recently, pad and paper in hand, and came up with several ideas for low-cost gifts. Here are only ten:

1. Two apples in gaily decorated bag with nifty apple-corer—$3.50.

2. Two lemons in a gaily decorated bag with a nifty lemon reamer—$3.20.

3. Bag of pretzels with jar of gourmet mustard (a must for my mom!)—$4.00.

4. Two cookie cutters tied together with twine, attached to dowel rolling pin—$7.50.

5. Gallon of cider, mulling spices, cinnamon sticks for package decoration—$8.00.

6. Bean soup mix in sturdy jar, dinky colorful ladles attached—$6.00.

7. Cooling rack with assortment of kitchen gadgets attached—$10.00.

8. Coffee mug filled with coffee beans—$8.00.

9. A half dozen bagels with bagel cutter—$8.00.

10. Pancake mix, maple syrup, pancake flipper—$8.95.

Once I roll up my sleeves and use some of the principles from the chapter on gift presentation, I will be off and running! You could do the same thing in a hardware store, a sporting goods store, a pet store, a stationery store, a craft store, a bookstore.

Food

There is a trend these days toward food-giving and happy are the people who receive! People *like* gifts of food.

- There is no denying: the all-time, no-fail gift for just about any occasion comes from the oven.

- Each year our family moves more in the direction of giving food. This past Christmas saw many baskets and packages of spices, fruit, coffee, candy, soups, cheese, and baked goods.

• As part of a wedding gift, I recently baked and then "built" a tower of hundreds of Italian biscotti (cookies) which was served at the reception. Pretty ribbons were incorporated in the tower, which was topped by a bouquet of fresh flowers.

• I try to keep a loaf of homemade bread in the freezer as special thanks for a telephone lineman or a repairman, or for an unexpected visitor.

• Food is the best gift in the world for college students and bachelors.

Let Me Count the Ways

There is more than one way to give. For starters, you can bring food *to* people:

Spaghetti Ministry

For some time, Joe and I had a secret operation going. We called it our "Spaghetti Ministry." We canned big batches of homemade tomato sauce and covered the canning lids with pretty red calico and ribbon. A jar of sauce, a package of spaghetti, a loaf of French bread, and an unsigned note were put in a small box. Off we drove to the house of someone we knew was in need or hurting emotionally. After Joe sneaked to the door and put down the box, he would run like blazes back to our car. (Once he was chased by a big, ugly dog.) Then we would speed away. The note just told the receiver that someone cared.

Special Dinners

An absolute favorite gift is presenting our toaster-sized recipe box with a red bow on top. We ask the birthday or anniversary celebrants to pick three recipes from the hundreds in the box. The only catch: they cannot pick recipes previously picked. At an appointed time, we go to their home and cook the meal! We have had rip-roaring disasters, a lot of fun, and always have a backup pizza in the freezer.

A variation to the special dinner could be to present someone with a cookbook (used or new) in which a red ribbon marks a favorite recipe that you have prepared.

Yet another variation is what we did with our dessert cookbook, which used to just sit with all the other cookbooks. One day we took it off the shelf and wrote on the inside cover:

> Dear Friend:
>
> Cookbooks, like friendships, sometimes sit on shelves and don't get used. Let's do something about that! Would you kindly look through this book and choose a recipe that appeals to you? Return the book, make note of the recipe, and we will prepare it for you.
>
> Joe & Cynthia

Bring Someone to Your Home

Here's an idea for those who want to do something for an entire group or family:

We have friends who have three active, primary-aged, school children. Wife and husband are professionals, who manage to attend school functions and to ferry their kids to every child activity on earth. These are busy people! We try to invite them to our home every few months to give mom one night off, to sit them all down to a home-cooked meal, and then to send them home to do homework.

Signature Gifts

The category "food" is so vast, I recommend you invent a few "signature gifts" which are easy, perhaps different, popular, and unique to you as a cook. What is it that you bake or cook or create? Turn that into a gift idea. Let me share mine: bread, Cheese Cracker Stew, popcorn balls, Mama's Brownies, and birthday cakes.

Bread: I like to make bread and do so several times each month. People enjoy receiving a loaf or two.

Cheese Cracker Stew: This is a Christmas tradition, one that could land me in big trouble if I failed to produce! Tins, jars, plastic sacks, or mugs are filled with this, which is gobbled at gulp speed.

CHEESE CRACKER STEW

Recipe: In double-strength plastic grocery sack combine the following: two boxes generic cheese "nips," one box oyster crackers, 1/2 cup oil (preferably popcorn oil), 2 packages dry buttermilk-ranch dressing, dill weed, lemon pepper (optional). Mix, mix, mix. Let sit overnight. Next day, divvy up.

Popcorn Balls: What an excellent gift this is! The recipe is easy enough for a child (with supervision), and the results are extraordinary. Here's what to do: Place each popcorn ball in a baggie and close it at the top with colorful curly ribbon. Put ten to twelve popcorn balls in a white cellophane bag (purchased from bakery) about twice the size of a lunch sack. Fold over the top of each bag and punch two holes. Thread white, red, or green "paper" ribbon through the holes, and tie in a huge bow in front of the bag. Underneath the bow, using a fat-tipped gold "paint" pen, write names of recipients in flowing cursive. (All of this without a glue gun, mind you!)

POPCORN BALLS

Recipe: Fill about 3/4 of a roasting pan with popped popcorn. In large pan, on low heat, melt one stick of margarine. Add 10-12 ounces of marshmallows. Melt and stir to make a nougat. Pour evenly over popcorn. *Important:* mix this as best you can with a big wooden spoon and then let it sit for about five minutes. With buttered hands, shape into balls, place on counter and let sit several minutes before putting in baggies.

Mama's Brownies: Use your favorite brownie recipe. We use one we found in Mama's recipe box after she died—it is a sure winner. Make a batch, wrap them individually, put them in a new brownie pan, and add an index card with the recipe. Send a note that the success of these brownies depends solely on using this special pan!

Birthday Cakes: I cannot understand why some people choose not to celebrate birthdays! Not only do I believe in birthdays as a celebration, I believe everyone should have a cake. I decorate small cakes especially for each recipient. At times I've even decorated a large muffin. When placed on a small, colorful plate and custom-tailored for a friend, a birthday cake (with a balloon or two) makes a great gift. It is one gift that says, "Hey, I remembered!"

Twelve Months of Christmas

One year I was at a loss for what to get an older couple dear to us. I invented the "Twelve Breads of Christmas." On a homemade card, I wrote a pledge to bake a different loaf each month. We are into our second year, and this present is appreciated over and over.

This can be used with nearly any food concept: soup, muffins, cookies, casseroles. Use your imagination. Bet you've thought of something already!

Spiritual

This category has two divisions: gifts for those *with* a spiritual nature, and gifts *of* a spiritual nature. There is a difference. Many of us—whom the world might call "religious"—are merely those who try to live life in reverence to God. Ours is a God-centered, or Christ-centered, life. Therefore, things that honor God or help us walk with him, are prized. For the spiritual person to cease being so would be the same as for the natural person to live without skin.

Gifts to Those With a Spiritual Nature

In a word: books. I know of no person with a spiritual nature who does not have lots of books. This is probably so for two reasons. One: Striving toward God-centered living, these people are attracted to anything that enhances their walk with him. And two: Seeking to know God better, spiritual people welcome any book that furthers their quest. This does not exclude humor or fiction! There is a delightful sense of humor in some biblical accounts, and the parables of Jesus could easily be called fiction-with-clout. There are books on philosophy, theology, and history. There are devotionals, meditations, books of inspiration, reference manuals, prayer books, and books on social issues. (One of the most provocative books I read this year was a tiny paperback on the history of Christian pacifism.) There are books that offer help during life crises, books that cheer people on, and hey—there are even books on frugal living and clever gift-giving!

Leah's Gift

My niece Leah once presented me with a gift that will probably go with me to my grave. It is a simple, homemade thing, I handle it every single day, and holding it gives me occasion to fondly think of her. It is a bookmark. With the help of her mom, Leah laminated a five-inch-long feather on top of a piece of yellow gingham wallpaper. There is nothing straight about the edges, cut so many years ago by four-year-old hands. On the back of this bookmark, in crayon, are the words "Merry Christmas 1991 love! Leah." When Leah presented me with this gift she told me the bookmark was for my Bible. And so it is.

Your Gift of You

When the Lord walked this earth, he told us to have a servant's heart. Many people are now turning to his instruction, and servanthood is seeing some revival. A gift of service—in someone's name—is indisputably one of the finest gifts you can give.

- A young husband recently rang a Salvation Army bell in the cold for three hours as a birthday gift to his wife. No question about that man's heart!

- Could you donate time on behalf of another? You needn't look far in your community, whether it be rural or inner city, to find a place where *your* heart is needed. Can you read to the blind, walk puppies at the pound, serve at a soup kitchen, clean a park, answer a phone, lick stamps, sit quietly with the dying, ring a bell?

- How about making a bookmark for your friend, your mate, your child, that pledges an hour each week or month toward one of these purposes? I bet it becomes a keepsake that is held with fond thoughts every single day!

- Can you fast for a period of time on someone's behalf?

There's More

Every year I give Leah and Olivia an empty box. Inside is a note informing each that money dedicated to them was spent on someone in need. This year Olivia gave a woman of limited means a shampoo and style, Leah gave a turkey. The girls understand. Grateful arms bear hug Uncle Joe and me—a double blessing.

Gifts of a Spiritual Nature

I urge careful consideration here. Some people, for a variety of reasons, reject the spiritual aspect of life. To barrage them with "religious stuff" can possibly create greater rejection of the Good News. So pray before you give!

A prayer from your *heart* (not from improper *motive*), can melt the heart of the hardest cynic. Let me tell you what I mean: From time to time I send someone the gift of prayer. I take pains to find (or make) a lovely card. On that card I write a prayer, using the person's name. I create a prayer from scratch which fits the person's circumstance, or I use a personal favorite from the Episcopal Book of Common Prayer. Let me share it with you now:

> Watch over thy child (person's name), O Lord, as her days increase; bless and guide her wherever she may be. Strengthen her when she stands; comfort her when discouraged or sorrowful; raise her up if she falls; and in her heart may thy peace which passeth understanding abide all the days of her life; through Jesus Christ our Lord. Amen.

Present this prayer with a single flower, either fresh or artificial. Pledge to pray the prayer for a specific period of time.

You could create a prayer for anyone, at any time, for any circumstance. How about an entire family? Write a specific prayer for each family member and include this one from the Prayer Book, written just for the care of children:

> Almighty God, heavenly Father, you have blessed us with the joy and care of children (here you could name the children). Give us calm strength and patient wisdom as we bring them up, that we may teach them to love whatever is just and true and

good, following the example of our Savior Jesus Christ. Amen.

I believe that even the most committed secularist would be moved to know you are on your knees daily in prayer for his or her children.

Romance

A woman came to me after I'd given a talk. Though undeniably a person of limited means, contentment and peace radiated from her spirit. She wondered if I would like to share her recent experience with others. I do so now, with the same heart-stirrings I had then:

> My husband and I were in the mall, not buying anything, just looking. We were separate for awhile, and as I window-shopped, I felt a gentle tug on my hand. It was my husband.
>
> "I want to show you something," he said.
>
> He led me to the card shop, down its crowded aisles, and stopped in front of the "Anniversary" section. The next day would be our anniversary, and my heart pinched at the thought of no money for even a card. My husband was clearly excited and almost reverently reached to pick the most beautiful card I'd ever seen. The cover of the card was raised in an explosion of flowers, the colors dazzling. He handed me the card to read. "If I could afford a card for you, Honey," he said, "this is the one I would buy."

The best romantic gifts are gifts you *cannot* afford: what is the price of your heart? of kindness not deserved? of forgiveness for an inconsiderate remark? of humor in a frustrating situation? of respect during a time of disappointment?

How to Be Romantic

People who are in love *want* to do things for their loved one. That is what being in love is all about. I've joked to our son about how to know if a young woman is interested. "She will make you cookies, Josh." There is truth to that. Molly came along and baked banana bread! When we love we can't wait to give. And though our giving is without expectation, it is nice when the object of our *amour* responds in kind.

Isle of View

I think that the two key elements of romantic giving are spontaneity and surprise. Let me tell you about our gift sack. It is one of those white paper sacks with a paper handle from the produce department at the market. The words "Isle of View" (I love you) are written on the sack with blue magic marker. The current holder of the sack is responsible for the next "sack attack." Joe has it now. Some day, when I am least expecting it, I will walk to my car, or pull back the bed covers, or reach for a pan—and I will find the sack. It might have a love note inside. Or a favorite candy bar. Or a meaningful gift. It once came taped to a box of spaghetti plates that caught my eye when we were out strolling. In the category of romance, gifts-for-no-reason-at-all bear the most significance.

Romantic Notions

Some things we have done:

- For my husband's thirty-third birthday, I wrote a pledge or sentiment on thirty-three cards. I presented my gift at our favorite spot. "One backrub, on demand," was his favorite.

- If you don't have a favorite spot, go exploring and claim one for the two of you. Maybe it will be a monument, a park alongside a body of water, a table at a coffeehouse, a scenic vista. A place to go to catch your breath or clear your minds is important to a relationship.

- Exchange roles for awhile. Joe ends up doing this when I am faced with a deadline: he becomes chief cook and bottle washer. A few hours ago he pinched his hand in the vacuum, overwatered a plant and made a flood, and tripped over a dog. I looked up from my work. "It's not so easy being a woman, is it?" was my cool, and teasing, remark ... but what a gift!

- Plant a tree on your anniversary. If you don't have a yard, find where you can plant by calling the Federal or State Forestry Department or the City Parks Department. Talk to a church committee or a friend who has land. What a thrill to know that "your" tree grows someplace in Virginia ten years later when you live in Montana.

- Compliment your mate in front of others. And mean it.

Keepsakes

One important criteria to keep in mind when searching for presents is how long interest will last, and how long the gift itself will last. I like to give keepsake, or long lasting, gifts.

Though this could have appeared under the Spiritual category, I saved the best keepsake gift for here: a Bible. There is no other gift I know that has more endearing, lifelong meaning than that of a good, quality Bible. If you doubt my words, look on the laps of the elderly when you visit a church, or look at the worn Bible on the stand next to Grandma's rocker. Bibles soon become highly personal and treasured. I could easily replace mine, but in the event of fire, my Bible is the first thing I would grab on my way out the door.

Will It Last?

When buying something you hope to be a keepsake, you must always consider quality. For instance: last year I purchased high quality birch recipe boxes for Olivia and Leah. I bought them with an eye toward their eightieth birthdays! Through the years each box will be jammed with recipes and sentimental memorabilia. To give them a jump-start, I included several recipes from family members.

A box, by the way, or any kind of interesting and sturdy container, makes a terrific keepsake gift, as does a good quality tin or small, covered basket. Every single person has a small treasure tucked away in *something*. Many of us remember having a cigar box held together with rubber bands. Looking around me now, I see at least six boxes in my office alone—some that have been "in the family" for over sixty years!

Heirlooms

I have my eye on an old serving spoon of my mother's. It used to belong to my grandmother. For all I know, it came

from Poland. I want that spoon. Value on the open market?
Zero. To me? Immeasurable.

- A family heirloom should be given only after some realistic
  calculation: Will it be preserved within the family? Will it be
  cared for? Will it be appreciated? Will it be passed to another
  generation? If these criteria are met, what could be a finer
  gift? Two years ago, we gave Josh his great-grandfather's
  gold watch, chain, and fob. It came from England and bears
  the inscription: "J.W. Yates, From His Young Men's Class,
  St. John's, Bolton, August, 1911." Josh was deeply touched—
  and promptly instructed us to return the watch to our safe
  deposit box!

- Do you have a piece of furniture, a bowl, a picture, a book, a
  piece of jewelry that can be passed to the next generation? It
  was touching when Joshua brought Molly home to propose
  to her using his grandmother's ring. It was so worn and thin
  that Molly would not dare to wear it, but the connection was
  made. Joshua brought the past, the present, and the future
  together when he slipped that ring on her finger. Hopefully
  it will continue to be significant to future generations of
  Yateses.

- It is a good thing to pass things on.

More Good Things

- Great idea for young adults: starter tool set. Actually, starter
  *any*thing!

- Jewelry, or special key chain. For his eighteenth birthday we
  presented Josh with a silver key chain inscribed with the following: "God first, others next, you last."

- Photos. A prized possession in this house is a black and white shot of Joe's dad (who *was* a cowboy!) after he'd been "dumped" by a bronco. Approximate age of photo: seventy-five years.

- A special piece of furniture. Years ago we bought Josh a bookshelf made from cherry wood. We also gave him a huge oak dresser that is covered with carvings. Might sound silly to give a ten-year-old an antique but guess what? The toys are long gone, the "boy" is grown—and the bookcase is still filled with favorite books.

Something Else Lasts a Lifetime

Teach someone a skill. Can you fish, sew, build, play piano, cook, paint, fix cars, clean, *read?* Teach another! Can you laugh? Teach someone! What greater gift than to pass along a skill—or a virtue—for another to use for life. I'd sure call that a keepsake!

Gift Certificates

I love to get gift certificates! There is something special about having one; it's like money in the bank. I amuse myself thinking of ways to spend my fortune—and plan my spending with the greatest care. This is a great gift idea!

But wait, you say, where is the creativity in THAT? Good question! Ready for some answers?

- One of the smartest –frugal—things you can give for Christmas is a gift certificate to a person's favorite store. Why? Remember the ornaments at 50 percent off? Most stores reduce prices drastically during the week between Christmas and New Year's. With careful use, a person could get up to twice as much (and buy what they want) during that week after Christmas. A twenty-dollar gift certificate can stretch a l-o-o-o-ng way in this circumstance.

- For Courtney and Glenn's wedding (our son's close friends) we marched all over town and scooped up gift certificates for everything we could think of: bagels at the bagel bakery, sandwiches at the deli, coffee at the bistro, fresh-cut flowers from the supermarket, lube, oil and filter, car wash, dinner at the Thai market, and others. We wanted to give the young couple *reasons* to go out, and the means to do it.

- Even during the tough years we were able to tuck five-dollar certificates to the Golden Arches in cards addressed to children.

- Present a child with an adventure gift certificate: take the child to the bakery, the meat market, a restaurant, a TV or radio station, a fire or police station, and explore *behind the scenes*. Tour a local business!

- Remember the shampoo and set Olivia gave? How was it handled? Anonymous gift certificate.

- Know of someone down on their luck? Do they own a car? Bet the oil needs changing. Bet you could buy a gift certificate. (The beauty of this is that it must be used specifically.)

- My mom has become an espresso hound. For her eightieth I slipped in a certificate for a few lattes from the drive-through vendor in town.

Gift certificates can be purchased from just about any kind of store or service. I've had them scrawled on the back of business cards—one store actually wrote the certificate on a shopping bag! I liked that. Right now I have one gift certificate to my name, for a free sundae at the local Tastee Freeze ... a close friend caters to my addiction to ice cream!

Homemade Certificates

A terrific idea! Make a "Queen for a Day" certificate and take your mom or friend shopping. Include lunch, a ride through the country ... and a trip to the Tastee Freeze.

When it comes to homemade, heaven is the limit. Caution: *Don't promise unless you're prepared to follow through.*

Registering Interest

A few years ago my family pitched in and put money on account for me at the kitchen gadget shop. Why? *On account* of the fact that I drool every time I go near the place! Any idea what it was like for me to browse and know *I could get practically anything I wanted?* Let me tell you, I was one happy cooker!

Do you know someone who has a very particular interest? Books? Fishing? Computers? Horses? Why not pitch in and put money on account at that person's favorite store ... *on account* of this being a very good idea!

There is one variation to this that I wish would catch on: Store owners tell me they would be happy to "register" people other than brides-to-be. Why not go into a store and write a list of different items you would appreciate? Family members (especially children and husbands) could read the list, check it twice, and then decide if *they* will be naughty or nice!

Tip: L.L. Bean, the catalog store with a rustic bent, has a Gift Registry in place. They encourage people to register their wish list with them so friends and family can order with confidence. For free information, call (800) 341-4341, ext. 3226.

Sentimental Collections

This category is not only fun, it makes a lot of sense, and in a way, takes some difficulty out of yearly gift giving: Add to someone's collection, or create a collection for someone.

- Remember my friend who likes things green and old? This makes scouting gifts easy for me. If I find anything reasonably priced that fits her collection, it's hers!
- Remember the ornaments my family gives one another? They aren't just any ornaments; Joe gives me either a crèche scene or an angel, I give him something rustic or from nature, we give Josh, and now Molly, something crafted with an "old-world" style.

Love-ly Ideas

- It began years ago when someone gave me a heart fashioned from dried flowers. I hung it on the wall near our bedroom ceiling, over our three mirrored closet doors. Soon others gave us hearts, which were hung on the wall. It turned into a collection, and hearts of every size and stripe came as gifts. We have covered a space ten feet long and two feet wide with hearts, each one a reminder of the loving heart who gave.
- Sister Sheila brings home a stein for Josh every time she visits Germany. They sit boldly on top of a bookcase, six at last count.
- Josh and Molly present each other with collector mugs from a favorite coffeehouse.

- Niece Olivia collects dog statues. Must be hereditary; I did that as a child. Mom still has a few of those critters collecting dust on her windowsills.
- Brother-in-law Rick is a numismatist. One Christmas present to him was a bright, shiny, OLD, silver dollar.

Tradition

Give the gift of tradition! I like to make traditions as much as I like to celebrate them.

- On May 7 Joe and I have breakfast for dinner—in celebration of our first meeting—at breakfast time.
- It would be a dismal Christmas indeed if I didn't give my mother a box of chocolate-covered cherries.
- Josh gets gummy bears regularly from Aunt Sheila—it is a gift of affection.
- I give Leah a bar of decorator soap at every gift-giving occasion. When she was a toddler she was fascinated by a bowl of small soaps in our bathroom.
- Sweet rolls for the people at Joe's office is a tradition in celebration of his birthday.

The Group Gift

There are times when several people can pool their funds or resources to give an expensive gift. When my family and friends pitched in to put a wad of dough on account for me at the kitchen gadget shop, I was delirious with excitement! What are some other ideas?

- Have you ever congregated with a group of people to paint someone's home? Or do home repair, say, for an elderly widow on a fixed income? Or make repairs for a single mom?

- The group gift is ideal for siblings. My sisters and I pooled our funds to take our mother to Calgary, Alberta, Canada for her eightieth birthday. We stayed at a bed and breakfast, went to ethnic restaurants, visited the Olympic site, attended a concert. What can you do for your mom and dad? Are they dreaming of an Alaskan cruise? Do they need a new TV?

- When Joe turned forty, I sent a note to all our friends. Rather than host a fortieth party, I "kidnapped" my husband and we rode the train to Seattle for a short holiday. Throughout our trip I reached into my purse and pulled out envelopes. One had two dollars from a friend with instructions to buy the morning paper. One had five dollars for a couple of es-pressos. One had money for lunch, another for a ride on the ferry, another for a loaf of French bread as we traipsed around Pike's Place Market. All wished him a fun-filled visit to Seattle, and the happiest of birthdays.

- Glenn is in graduate school, and typically broke. Glenn wrote a letter to friends and asked that we consider chipping in to buy his wife a camera for her birthday. No question about that young man's heart!

  Caution: Think carefully before you approach people to participate financially in a present (or an adventure!). To some, solicitation might be considered bad taste.

- Have a relative who hunts or fishes? Worry about him get-ting lost? Everybody pitch in and buy a Global Positioning System. This is a rather expensive gizmo that takes latitude and longitude positions on the ground from satellites. Helps Gramps find his way home—or to shore.

- Too hard for Gram to answer someone's call? Pool your funds and buy a portable phone. Maybe Gramps can call her from the woods and tell her he's OK!
- Have Mom and Pop made his-and-her craters in their old mattress? Get the family to pitch in and buy a new spring and mattress set. While you're at it, spring for a couple of good down pillows.

4

Package Pizazz and All That Jazz
EFFORTLESS WRAP WITH WHIMSY AND WARMTH

Know what? Presentation is everything! It's true: it doesn't matter *what* you are presenting, but *how*. Whether a handshake, a ride in your car, or a gift from your heart, as the French would say, *présentation, c'est tout!* [Presentation is everything!] Let me use the examples I just gave to bring home my point:

- Have you ever thought of your handshake as an extension of you? What do you say when you say hello with the palm of your hand? Is your hand clean? Are your nails trimmed? Do you grasp with a hearty grip and look someone in the eye? Is it a gift to offer your hand in greeting, in reconciliation, in sympathy? I think it is.

- If a ride in your car is more like a trip to Mars … or more like the *landscape* on Mars, you might need to work on presentation! You must remember that everything you wear, everything you own, everything you say is a reflection of you as a person. What are you saying when your car is loaded down with candy wrappers, banana peels, and junk mail?

- A gift from your heart will be appreciated, but so much more if you take the time to present it with care and thought.

Which would you rather receive: a gift in the store's plastic sack with the price still attached, or the same gift creatively wrapped and presented with flair?

I know, I know. Some of you are thinking that if it was up to you to wrap gifts, presentation would definitely NOT be everything! Your past efforts ended up looking as if the packages went through the bend, spindle, and mutilate machine at the post office. (We know it is there, don't we?) I can't give you the skill, but I can fill you with ideas. Some of the ideas in this chapter even offer an "easier" method to wrap—so you don't have to fret over those wicked corners any longer!

Alternatives

There are a few solid reasons for alternative gift wrap, but two head the list: cost and ecology. Think about this: You are in an unfamiliar town and need gift wrap for a wedding present *now*. Into the nearest card shop you charge and out you come with a package of wrapping paper and a matching bow. Average cost to you? Five dollars. Add a card for another three dollars. (This doesn't include the scotch tape you had to spring for, either.) Now, what happens to that paper? The bride and groom *rip* it off the package, don't they? What happens to the card? Sooner or later it gets tossed.

Now let's talk about ecology with one question: where does the stuff that gets tossed go? Answer: landfill.

So let's "wrap" this up. You pay a considerable amount of money for paper products that get ripped and thrown away and end up adding to the trash in our landfills.

Not only that, most store-bought wrap is predictable and boring, so …

Present-ing You With New Ways to Put Zip in Your Doo-Dahs!

1. Save any kind of paper that can be used to wrap a package:

- This morning I covered a huge pasta box with white butcher paper saved from a meat purchase. I used magic markers to gaily decorate the box with birthday greetings. Balloons and a big, fat red ribbon added to the excitement of my present. The recipient? A seven-year-old boy. What was the box filled with? Gaily decorated cupcakes.

- Recycle wrapping paper that comes on gifts you receive. Yes, I'm the one in my family who politely requests that Christmas presents be opened carefully. But I don't carry it as far as my friend who does everything but scrub her hands for brain surgery when she opens gifts!

- Tissue paper is the end-all, ultimate, low-cost, and versatile way to go! Save every piece of tissue paper you get. The drawback to tissue paper is that you can see through the stuff if you only use one sheet. This is great for those of you who are all thumbs in the gift wrap department, though, because it can be jammed into a pretty gift sack and the present stuffed inside.

- I have an *endless* supply of salmon-colored paper that came on a foot-thick roll. Our son used this paper to cover windows when he painted houses during college. Labels, colored ink, and ribbon bring elegance to packages wrapped with this paper.

- Use lining paper that comes as packing for objects shipped by mail, etc.

- Use an old road map or computer paper.

2. Use newspaper! I like to wrap books in newsprint:
   - The Sunday funnies are perfect for a children's gift, and look smashing with a big red ribbon.
   - Regular newsprint looks good with red ribbon, too.
   - Any chance you can get newspaper in a foreign language?
   - Spritz on hairspray to make the paper shine, but don't saturate it—and spray *before* you wrap.

   *A word of caution: years ago, when I wrapped in newsprint to "save the planet," I gave an elegant shower gift that was looked upon with surprise and some annoyance ... the wrapping was not only before its time, it didn't fit the occasion.

3. Wrap small items with attractive magazine pages. It is especially fun if you can find an advertisement that might match the gift in some way:
   - If you are giving perfume, wrap the gift in one of those scented perfume ads.
   - If giving a ring, find an ad showing hands, if earrings, use a picture of a model's head.
   - You could scout up something musical—or sheet music—to wrap something for a musician friend.

4. Some paper is just too flimsy for the job and you need industrial strength wallpaper. This is an inexpensive way to go, especially if you have a big, clunky object to wrap. Paint stores often have bins of this stuff on closeout.

5. Fabric can wrap a gift in more than one way:
   - Use a scrap of purple velvet to create an old-fashioned book cover. Sew the tucks with matching thread. Elegant.
   - Leftover pieces of calico with a matching ribbon make lovely presentations.

6. Brown or white grocery sacks (without printing) of every size can be used to hold gifts. Attach clever ribbons to make this easy method complete:

    *Go to the craft section of a big discounter and have a look at the different ribbons they sell. You will be astonished. Buy a few rolls of paper ribbon, raffia, or wired ribbon just to have on hand. Experiment with your next gift project. I bet you surprise yourself!

    • Rustic, but dynamite for presentation, is humble brown grocery sack paper.

    • Inside-out silver potato chip bags (cleaned of grease) make stunning presentations when tied at the top with bright ribbon.

7. Gift bags with handles are simple to present, and will usually be recycled by the recipient. Line the bag with tissue paper, fabric, Easter grass, or a new dishtowel, and add the gift. Tie the handles together with ribbon or pretty yarn and you have a dandy-looking present. Some store sacks come with handles. Save them! Wrap an iridescent wire laden with stars around the handle of a small sack and stick cookies inside.

8. Bunch colorful pillowcases at one end and tie with a ribbon to present basketballs, footballs, tackle boxes, and other awkward objects.

9. Pretty cotton dishtowels are terrific when wrapping bottles. Give someone a bottle of exotic grape juice for Christmas. Wrap in a colorful cotton towel and attach an enormous pine cone where it is gathered at the neck. Outstanding.

10. Use the object itself as the wrapper! One year I gave a cotton sweatshirt with a fun Southwestern pattern. I rolled

it "bedroll" fashion and "tied" it in two places with a couple of thin leather belts. The name tag was a piece of cardboard attached with twine.

11. A scarf or bandanna can be gathered as a bundle around an object.

12. Aluminum foil or colored Saran Wrap make great wraps in a pinch.

13. Wrap a gift in a homemade envelope of burlap. Use yarn or twine to sew the edges closed, attach a huge button on the end of the "envelope" flap to hold it down, insert gift inside. I did this with an old book, then wrapped a rawhide bookmark around the big button.

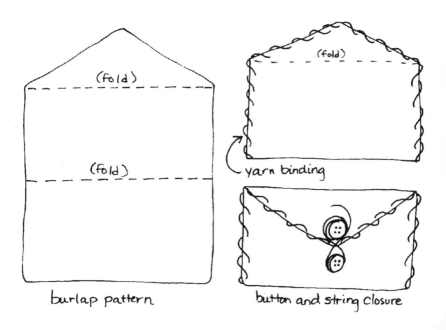

burlap pattern

button and string closure

Boxes

Have you bought a box from a store lately? It comes flat and you are supposed to assemble it at home. Problem is, you need a staple gun, super glue, and spray starch just to keep the corners from collapsing back to flat again! Once upon a time, boxes were strong and straight; now they are wimpy, thin, and accordion-like. What to do?

- Search your pantry. You will be surprised by the assortment of sturdy boxes you have lining your shelves. I cook the *strangest* meals on nights I'm gearing up for Christmas—just because I am hunting up boxes. Think of what you can do with an oatmeal box!

- Use the inside tubes from toilet paper, paper towels, and, yes, if you bought it, Christmas wrap. I heard of one woman who pinned together a long string of socks for her young daughter, then stuffed them into one of these long tubes. Imagine the delight of the child as she pulled out socks and more socks.

- Think of the size box you need, then think of the stores in town. Which store sells things the size of the box you need: shoe stores, grocery stores, appliance stores? Go ask for their empties.

- Wooden boxes are great, but kind of pricey. You could make the box the main gift, though.

- Tins make great containers. We try to give a new "old" tin to Josh and Molly each year.

Baskets R Us

Baskets are perfect containers! Imagination can be stretched to the farthest limits when considering presentation in a basket. Not only is the basket *itself* a gift, it can be used for a number of purposes. In our home we use them for toiletries, storing vegetables, kitchen utensils, papers, paper trash, pencils and pens, washcloths, magazines, and carryalls when we are off to someone's home with goodies.

The basket you give could continue to be an integral part of your gift. For instance, in our bathroom we have a multi-colored, sturdy Easter basket with a tall handle in which we have a dozen high-quality white washcloths, rolled and assembled standing up. This would be a darling new home or shower gift if it came with a loofah sponge or a couple of designer soaps on a delicate string dangling from the handle. Tie each washcloth with colorful cloth ribbon for extra verve.

Liners:

Baskets don't have to be lined, but some sort of liner adds dramatically to the presentation. I have lined baskets with:
- artificial grass for Easter
- new dish towels
- cloth napkins, fabric
- pine boughs/pine cones (especially small)
- Christmas garland (which can be wrapped around the handle!)
- crumpled tissue
- sod with rich green grass
- Styrofoam peanuts used for packing
- fall leaves

The Trick:

Try to find a basket that fits the gift, both in style and size. For instance, one of the neatest gifts I've seen was a fishing creel filled with lures, bug spray, and a book for the amateur naturalist. (Bug spray in a delicate little wicker basket would have looked mighty strange.) If you are trying to maximize the gift but minimize the expenditure, put one very large, inexpensive item in the basket to take up much of the room.

Tasty Ideas:

Food and baskets go together like love and marriage. Present one of these Epicurean delights to your friends:

- Wouldn't it be loverly if you presented a basket of ... potatoes! Why not? Buy good quality bakers, present them with a new potato peeler, a "French-fry" machine, a gravy skimmer, or a cookbook like *The Well-Dressed Potato*. Cover with a nice new dishtowel (your wrapping paper) and hang wooden veggies from the handle.
- A basket of popcorn balls plopped on top of pine boughs is gift enough. If you are generous you could include a microwave popcorn cooker or a jar of gourmet popcorn. Dangle an ornament or a pine cone from the handle.
- Cookies! And the bigger the better! Make mammoth cookies and pile them high. Include a cookie cookbook, a cookie mix, or a recipe. Cookie sprinkles would add whimsy and color. Hang a note from the handle that says this is the secret recipe of Cookie Monster. Tie two cookie cutters on each end of a six-inch long ribbon and wrap it around the handle.

- If you are certain you aren't going to wipe anyone out, send a basket of your home-canned produce. Line the basket with a small piece of calico, then use calico to cover the lids. Cut a round piece of calico using the lid as your guide. Just cut two inches wider all around. Place calico on lid, then screw on the band. Include a package of canning labels. Attach a small wooden spoon to the handle.

- Pasta to go! Never mind chocolate; *this* is the stuff of romance. Find an oblong bread basket and tie a fistful of spaghetti with thick red yarn. Include an Italian cookbook, some good olive oil, seasoning, or a cheese grater. Use the same yarn to tie a spaghetti ladle to the side.

- Man can give the *gift* of bread alone! And your homemade bread needn't be humongous. At times, I make three "mini" round loaves out of one batch of bread dough. This is especially effective when I make a heavy, whole grain bread. Bread always looks good nested in a dish towel or huge napkin that can be pulled up over the top. Include a mix, a bread knife, a dough scraper.

- OLÉ! How about a festive basket filled with the Southwest? You could include a box of taco shells, taco spice, fry bread mix, salsa, and hot sauce. Hang dried chilies from the too-hot-to-"handle."

- Soup's on! A favorite "welcome back to the lake" gift for friends is a small, fabric-lined basket that has enough room for a jar of homemade soup and a few rolls or goodies. You could include soup mix, a mug, herb blends, and a pot-holder. Hang tiny plastic ladles from the handle.

- This was a gift for my sister Anne last year: I put several varieties of rice in their own baggies, tied the top with colorful yarn, and pasted a name label on each one. These packets went into a low, flat basket, along with chopsticks and rice bowls. A separate gift was a microwave rice cooker.

- I know I'm not the only coffee snob in the world—I love to get a bag of beans! Coffee and tea make terrific gifts, especially for the one-who-has-it-all. Include flavored powdered creamers, mugs, a new teapot. Maybe stick in a couple of biscotti—those neat Italian dipping cookies.

- An apple a day keeps the "What-do-I-*get?*"-blues away! Nothing at all wrong with a basket of red and green apples, especially if they are shiny and bright. Include a fancy new corer and caramel dip. Tie two cinnamon sticks to the handle with raffia.

- Bon voyage! Give your friend a *good*bye with an oblong basket that includes two travel mugs, some bread, cheese, or cookies.

Alternatives to Baskets

Enough with the basket, already! *You* want to do something different! Read on.

- Stick your gift in a new baking pan or pot. A stainless-steel stew pot offers endless possibilities.

- Does your friend like old bowls? Find one and fill it with potpourri, spring flowers, or candy.

- Attach inexpensive and colorful gadgets to the grid of a roasting rack or a cooling rack.

- Stick gardening gadgets or seed packets inside a flower pot. Tie an enormous raffia bow to the pot. Make sure something is sticking up high into the air, like a wooden crop marker.

- A lowly *sandwich bag* looks terrific with curly ribbon and bells or buttons. What can you give in a sandwich bag? Cookies or penny candy! I was in a pinch one day and purchased a dozen day-old cookies from a gourmet bakery. I tied lots of curly ribbon around the twist-tie closure and that was enough to dazzle my friend.

- Tins cannot be beat … best filled with imaginary or chocolate kisses!

- Go to the thrift store and think *cookies*. Look at each plate, platter, or tin they have. Look for the unusual. Pile cookies on your "find" and cover with colored Saran Wrap.

- A Christmas stocking can carry lots of good cheer.

- Find a high-quality wooden recipe box and fill it with favorite recipes.

- I read about a dungaree *pocket* filled with jelly beans and stuffed with a colorful red bandanna. (No pants, just the pocket.) You could cut the pocket from worn-out jeans, wash, and finish the edges.

- Why can't a cuddly teddy bear bear the gift—like a necklace, a pin, a watch.

Decorations Even a Klutz Can Manage

We've talked about gift wrap, we've talked about boxes and containers and baskets. Now we are going to talk about the finishing touches to your gift. We're going to add a little pizazz.

People are forever coming up to me and saying something like, "It's fine for *you* to talk about all of this, but what about those of us who aren't very creative?" I immediately remind them of my fiasco with the glue gun. Then I tell them that decorating—a package or a table for dinner—is as simple as opening drawers and taking things out. It really is. You needn't be intimidated. Just always try to "color outside of the lines." Try to do something a little differently. I guarantee that you will surprise yourself.

There are a few things to take into consideration: color schemes, theme, holiday, type of wrap on the gift itself. You would not want to have competing colors on a package. Color can be used to draw attention or to convey a feeling. For instance, did you know that in Africa, gifts wrapped in red symbolize wishes for good health? In green, for wealth. (Makes you think about our red and green color combination for Christmas, doesn't it?)

Think of the reason for the gift. Remember my expensive shower gift wrapped in common newspaper print? It was a dud. If I remember correctly, it didn't even have ribbon. Think about the occasion and then proceed with decoration accordingly. Tiny flags might adorn a birthday around the Fourth of July, tinsel a gift around Christmas, rice might look good glued to the top of a wedding gift. If your present is a pick-me-up for a depressed friend, stay quiet on the wrap and add a touch of color to the ribbon. (When I'm down, the last thing I need is a cheerleader dressed in day-glo pink doing a jitterbug in my face.)

Look at the basic gift wrap. Is the print so busy you hardly need ribbon? Would too many gizmos on the top take away from the elegance of the paper itself? Is the paper dull (like my painting paper) and does it invite as much flair as you can muster?

Putting Punch in Your Paper

- I have a few marker pens that write in gold. I use fine point on cards, and medium on the gift itself. At times, I simply write the name of the person across the top of a gift in the most flowing handwriting I can muster.
- A doily can be used as a stencil. Place it on plain gift wrap. Lightly dust with spray paint, and let it dry before you remove the doily.
- Slice vegetables lengthwise (carrots) or in half (onion) and dip in acrylic paint. Use as you would a sponge and make veggie shapes all over the paper.
- Carve a design in a potato and use it as a stamp. Dip in acrylic paint.
- Use a sponge. Cut into any shape you wish, dip in acrylic paint. Let me tell you what I did to an eight-inch square box: I crumpled a brown paper sack into a tight wad, then smoothed it out on the table (the creases were still there). I cut a sponge into the shape of a cactus and used green acrylic paint to stamp cacti all over the paper. After I wrapped the box, I "tied" it up with baling twine, and attached a small wooden cactus (thrift store) to the twine.
- Use rubber stamps to create a design.
- Glue glitter on the paper.
- Use stickers to decorate.

More Punch

The rest of this book could be filled with suggestions for adorning a package. Here are just a few to get your creative juices flowing:

- Use shoelaces, twine, yarn, or string instead of ribbon.
- Glue buttons in a decorative pattern or in the person's name on the box.
- Cut a doily into pie-shaped forms and separate slightly. Glue on box.
- I like to use old-fashioned gift labels on presents. When I use a decorative gift label I rarely present a greeting card. For a good source for labels and stickers, write to Dover Publications, 31 East 2nd Street, Mineola, NY 11501. Ask for a catalog.
- Do you needlepoint? Why not adorn a package or a jar with one of your latest creations?
- Make a quilt design of leftover fabric and glue it to a box. (Yes, sigh, a glue gun would definitely come in handy in this chapter!)
- Make a collage of magazine photos and glue it to box.
- Use alphabet noodles to spell out a message or a name.
- Small bells add jingle to any package.
- Paint a wishbone with nail polish and use to adorn a "wishful" gift … like a box with an engagement ring inside.
- Attach blown-up balloons to a package.

Doodads

This is unlimited, even for a limited imagination! Try to add a little trinket or gadget on top of your gift that might hint of what's inside. A gift for a cook? Attach a whisk. For a baby? A rattle. A carpenter? A thick pencil. Get it?

Greeting Cards

There is a troubling lack of civility in our world today; in our language, in our dress, in our manners. We've drifted away from gentler times when we took time to honor someone, whether with our appearance or our sentiments. A crisp piece of white paper, careful handwriting, and a heartfelt message will *always* be more meaningful to the recipient than even the prettiest greeting card if all you do is sign your name. It is much too easy to drift into a card store and spend a few dollars. There is no question that a personal note can be taxing on the brain, so read on for some help in the homemade-greeting-card department.

The Simple

Go to a stationery store or a major discounter and spend time looking for a package of blank note cards that fit your personal style in size, texture, and color. You may want your signature card to sport some sort of design. You may want a zippy color integrated into your card or envelope. You may want a small note card. I prefer a large, blank, white card, made out of a heavier-than-usual paper. This is perfect because it allows *my* choice of design: I can jazz it up with an old-fashioned sticker, I can make it quiet by using simple black scroll, I can use colored ink with a flourish. These note cards are big enough for me to convey any sort of message and feeling.

All That Jazz

- Use a glue stick to paste a photo on the front. Sending holiday greetings to a distant relative? Paste a crazy picture of him at the barbecue when he visited last summer.

- Paste a picture from a magazine on the front. Magazine *covers* are heavier paper stock, and offer an endless supply of ideas for card decoration and theme. One of my all-time favorites was a picture of young children, brilliant with color. Made a great birthday card for Grandma.

- Paste *words* from a magazine. Browse until you find just the right word or sentence. Glue away. I found the words "It all starts with a seedling" in a forestry ad. Pasted it on a note of congratulations to a mother-to-be.

- Paste something of sentimental value to the recipient. Want to remind a friend of the good times you had? Plaster the front of the card with your theater ticket stubs.

- Use colorful labels or stickers. I am fond of a simple presentation: I position a flower sticker in the upper left corner on the front, and address the recipient in gold cursive writing just below.

front   inside

- Decorate the front with a rubber stamp; use different colored ink pads. My friend Jo is a wizard with these things, using seasonal theme stamps on everything she sends out, even her bills!
- An elegant piece of ribbon, or a small dried flower, can be glued to your card. Don't ever be afraid to do something daring!
- Children's crayons can be used with whimsical results.
- Children's watercolor paint sets work well, too.

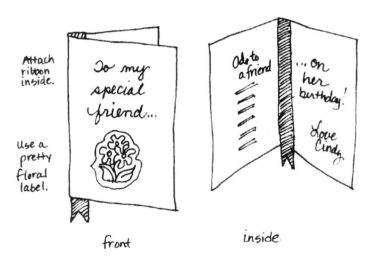

Attach ribbon inside.

To my special friend...

Use a pretty floral label.

front

Ode to a friend

...on her birthday!

Love Cindy

inside

The Silly Card

A favorite production for this family is to sit around the table with colorful construction paper, glue, scissors, and a stack of magazines and junk mail. We fold several pieces of construction paper in half, "book" size, and then begin creating a humorous tale about the recipient, complete with picture and word illustrations that we cut from magazines. We end up howling, as does the person who gets one of these masterpieces. Try it! It works particularly well for a young person who is courting.

Juvenile Cards

When a young child is celebrating a birthday, create a card with construction paper folded in half lengthwise. On the face of this write HAPPY BIRTHDAY, using the child's name. Do this with magic markers that smell like candy. Inside the fold, tape coins and uninflated balloons and an assortment of wrapped candies. Keep a stash of bigger-than-usual envelopes just for this purpose. Decorate the envelope with stickers.

The Sublime Card

Just the other day we sent a card to a high-school graduate who plans to attend photography school. What did we write? Why, "CONGRADUATIONS!" of course, with the inside saying "We hope your life is filled with Kodak moments!" You can fashion a card like that, too.

If you are at a complete mental standstill, turn to Psalms, a book of poetry, or cards *you've* received for inspiration.

Sympathy Cards

In my opinion, there is *nothing* more insensitive at a time of loss than a store-bought condolence card that is merely signed. This is one time when you must take time to care. If you are using a store card, write something besides just your name. Best, though, if you express your deepest sympathy and extend an offer to help.

Some time ago, little Stephanie's kitten Chloe was killed by a car. Stephanie's grandmother told me the girl was filled with sorrow. I marched home and wrote a card in book form. I told Stephanie how sorry I was, and page after page, I encouraged her to do different things: tell her mother why Chloe made her happy, draw a picture of Chloe, draw a picture of what sad felt like, and as the book progressed, I asked Stephanie to do hopeful things: to talk with her dad about what she would do when she came to the lake, to think about boating with Grandpop.

Family Project: Christmas Card

Get together with your kids and design a card on a sheet of typing paper. Write your message, sign your names. Use crayons, markers, stickers. Search out the least expensive photocopy service in town and splurge an extra penny for colored paper. Hand-decorate each of your envelopes or fold the paper in thirds and close with a colorful sticker. I bet your homemade card ends up on someone's refrigerator!

5

Tots and Teens and In-Betweens
WHAT TO GET THE KIDS

I know. They all want toys. And that's OK: toys and kids were made for each other. There are times that nothing but—and I mean *nothing but*—a particular toy (even in a particular color, mind you!) will fit the bill. If you think back to your own childhood, no doubt you will bang into a memory that causes a stir inside of you, and a smile as you remember the sweet, sweet moment when you unwrapped *it*. Was it a doll, a toy bulldozer, a wagon? My husband Joe still cherishes the memory of his pedal-driven fire truck. Me? A saddle for my pony, Princey.

Satisfying every want and desire of a child is unhealthy, but a very hoped-for gift that will cause a stir in a child's heart and a smile on *your* face is a good thing.

Want some creative alternatives to that particular something? Here are *nothing but* terrific ideas for youngsters:

Infants
This is an easy category because the baby hasn't yet learned there is such a thing as a return policy at the local store. Infants also do not care if you present them with underwear, patent

leather beach hats, or sensible shoes. As long as they can chew on something and drool, life is good.

There are two gift categories here: for the child, and, in reality, for the parents. Let's talk about the child first.

Lasting Gifts—Monetary

- Savings bond. This is a favorite gift, one that can be repeated throughout the child's life. For instance, our son Joshua presents his godson and namesake with a bond on his birthday. When little Joshua goes to college, gets married, has children of his own, or runs into a financial crunch, he will bless the socks off his godfather, guaranteed. Please don't think you have to keep giving bonds: this may just be a sensible, one-time gift.

- Mutual funds or stocks. Don't be frightened by this. If you check around, you may find a fund that will take small, incremental investments. We have every intention of checking with a stockbroker when our grandchildren come along. We most certainly will treat the children to an occasional "Grandpa-I-will-*die*-without-this!" present, but our aim is to give gifts that will outlast the fire trucks and pony saddles.

- A personal savings account. There is no reason you couldn't designate a special piggy bank for a special child and fill it year-round. Empty it on the child's birthday and make a deposit in the child's account.

- A silver dollar or a gold piece might be an impressive present for a baby ... if you think the parents will not spend it!

Lasting Gifts—Non-Monetary

- A locket with the child's initials. Perhaps a baby ring or a bracelet with the name engraved. Please use extreme caution if considering anything that might cause choking or injury to a child. Small jewelry pieces are often used for ceremony alone and then stashed as sentimental objects.

- Monogrammed silver utensils for children or a silver drinking cup.

- Monogrammed teething ring.

- One of the finest ideas I've heard of: family and friends purchase flatware settings for the child. Utensils are engraved with the name of the relative, such as, "Aunt Anne," "Uncle Will," "Cousin Alexandra," "Your Big Brother Glenn." I love this idea! Think of the smiles this will evoke when the child grows and sets her table.

- A handcrafted item made especially for the child. When Josh was an infant, a friend's mother gave him a ceramic rabbit. When old enough to talk, Josh dubbed it "Runny Babbit," and do you know, that silly old rabbit still sits on his shelf! It once served as a bookend to Winnie the Pooh, now it sits next to Plato's *Republic*.

- Newspaper from the day of birth. Better yet: make a scrapbook of the day the child was born, using newspapers and magazines as sources.

- A letter. How special for a grandparent or special friend to write a personal letter to the newborn—maybe something to be read on the child's twelfth, or eighteenth, or twenty-first birthday!

- A first teddy bear! I saw this great idea on TV: Convince great-grandma to part with her fur piece and bring it to a seamstress. Or make the bear yourself. High marks in sentiment for *this* idea.

- A journal. My husband, Joe, had the joy and privilege to stand as best man for our son's marriage to Molly. Josh and Molly gave my husband a leather-bound journal. Josh asked his father to write notes to his future grandchildren, about life, about family, and about his love of the Lord. I smile through gentle tears as I write this, knowing full well that one of my husband's clear admonitions in that journal will be "never burn your chopping block!"

- A family heirloom. Don't have one? Create one! And create one for each child. In my husband's family, the immense family Bible is given to the firstborn son of the firstborn son, and so on. It sits in our home and technically belongs to Josh, then to his first son. You can do the same thing, but with each child. Find an old pitcher or photo that gets handed down to the firstborn daughter, or the second son or the third daughter. You could even use …

- A Christmas ornament! What gift has more lasting value and memory than a special ornament either crafted with the child in mind, or bought to last?

Baby Gifts—Clothes

Even though we ooh and aah over infant chic, the standard garb of diaper, undershirt, sleeper, and blanket lead the baby fashion hit parade. Practical and washable are important features to add to other thoughtful clothing *do's and don'ts*.

- Consider if this is the first baby, or if there are other children, and if they are the same gender. If there will be a lot of hand-me-downs, it might make sense to purchase some other type gift.

- Consider the climate and environment where the child will normally live. If a country setting, there may be a greater call for outdoorsy clothing.

- Are the mom and dad naturalists who prefer all-natural, cotton or wool clothing?

- Will it make more sense for you to buy a toddler snowsuit for the July baby? Or a fleece sleeper? Believe me, warm clothes are appreciated when temperatures start to fall.

- Consider bonnets and hats for the child living in a sunny place.

- *Always* consider ease in dressing a child. Will the mother have to hold the baby upside down and lower him into your outrageous outfit? Will the dad need a crowbar and axle grease to wiggle his daughter into that to-die-for captain's suit you found?

- Did you have a favorite outfit for one of your babies? Try to find the same thing.

- Many consignment shops offer higher-end quality children's clothing. And many of you have hand-me-downs taking space in your home. Put together a box of crisp, clean, and pressed clothes. Most moms won't mind a bit. You may want to check this out first, though, because you would not want to offend someone. This *is* a gift, after all!

- As noted before, if you know you will be needing a baby gift, watch for end-of-season and baby week sales. Think ahead. (Having a plan will help you immensely.) Buy in advance in a neutral color and stash the gift away.

- Whether purchasing on sale or for full retail, if you are buying something a bit out of the ordinary, be certain there is a return policy. But please, please keep something in mind: the last thing the mother of a little baby needs is to run around exchanging gifts.

- For older siblings: a T-shirt with some sort of statement printed. For example, "I am Megan's older sister."

- Bibs, bibs, and more bibs.

- A terry cloth bathrobe, with a hood, is indispensable at any age.

Diapers

These things deserve a space all their own. Nothing can be more appreciated—especially if the child will be using disposables—than a box of diapers. Sometimes our gift is a case load. It may not tickle the fancy as much as a frilly dress, but if you've ever needed these things you know I'm right. A certificate for a diaper service would be nice, too.

Baby Gifts—Other Things

- Babies need *stuff*. Stuff like strollers, cribs, portable cribs, diaper bags, car seats, bottles, changing tables, and diaper pails. Any of the above can be found at the bigger chain discounters or at warehouse stores. *Anytime* you buy *anything* for a child, *always* consider safety. Particularly beware of lead paint that might cover an old find.

- A sunshade for the car window is one of the most thoughtful gifts! Also, baby-sensitive sunscreen lotion.
- How about a non-skid tub seat for bathing?
- Life preserver if the child will be on or near the water.
- There are slings on the market today that put baby in front of mom or dad, resting up against the chest. This keeps both hands free and baby close to your heartbeat.
- Buy a case or two of infant formula or baby food. Check with mom first.

For Parents

- In a word: money. No, *that* isn't very creative, but I betcha most dads would welcome any extra income at a time like this. That Gerber Baby cooing in their lap is going to set them back a bundle, beginning now.
- Gift certificate for dinner out—and you baby-sit!
- Baby-sit for no reason at all. Offer to watch the child/children for one afternoon each month, for an hour every Wednesday morning, for a weekend reprieve. Mothers welcome this chance to catch up with necessary chores, and dads welcome a chance for the couple to concentrate on themselves for an uninterrupted time.
- Offer to accompany a parent on a shopping trip … or anyplace else, for that matter. You watch the child while mom tries on some new clothes. You burp the baby when it starts fussing in a restaurant. You cradle the infant in the crying room at church and give the parents a chance to get through the service in peace.

- A small grinder so Mom can make baby food at home is a welcome tool, as is an *easy-to-clean* warmer plate. Think convenience. How about a baby food cookbook?
- A smoke alarm, a baby monitor—or an ABC rated fire extinguisher. (I'm a firm believer that parents should have the latter next to their bed, along with a flashlight.)
- Find a source for picture frames and buy several sizes. Be sure to include a couple of clear Lucite picture holders with magnetized backs for the refrigerator.
- Give the mom a certificate for a manicure. Give the dad a certificate for a massage.
- A pretty spray of flowers.
- Don't just stand there with a gift, DO something! Wash clothes, iron, clean a house, wash windows, *make dinner.*

Toddlers—Clothes

Clothing gifts make a lot of sense for these munchkins. Consider something when making your selection: parents still have to dress the child, who is now *active*. Add to this the fact that the active child crawls and falls. Never mind those cowboys on the range; denim was created with toddlers in mind! When my son was a toddler I began to pay serious attention to proper attire, from head to toe. I was certain to buy good shoes for my son's developing feet and winter jackets that protected his neck and his lower back.

- Pants with knees that have reinforcements or patches. One enterprising woman sewed patches on patchless toddler pants (and worn-out knees on pants) as a gift for a young mom.

- One-piece snowsuits that are warm but supple so junior doesn't look like he's made out of cardboard when he tries to walk.
- For winter, find a Polarfleece hat that snaps under the chin and covers the neck from the cold. For summer, find a breathable hat that also protects the neck from sunburn.
- Raincoat and rubber boots. Is there a child alive who doesn't splash in puddles? Why not tie on a small, colorful umbrella when you decorate the package of boots and coat?
- Joshua practically *lived* in his one-piece, head-to-toe sleeper that zipped up the front.
- The very latest in training pants.
- A sweater or sweatshirt that zips or closes with Velcro. And doesn't itch.
- A pretty apron designed to protect a frilly dress.
- Mittens by the carload. Don't give gloves: they are too hard to put on and they aren't warm anyway. Get those with Thinsulate, if possible, for toasty warm fingers.
- A terry cloth bathrobe.

Toddlers—Other Things

- A "cool" pair of sunglasses.
- A wooden spoon and a couple of old pots.
- As awful as this may sound to some of you—a child-safety harness. Very young children wander and that is unsafe. Twenty-five years ago, a child on a "leash" (as I called them) seemed reprehensible to me. If I had a child today and went shopping alone with the child, I would have a death grip or a harness on him.

- A big ball.
- A set of keys that cannot possibly, under any circumstance, come apart from the key holder.
- An activity set for the car seat.
- Books written with very young children in mind: picture books with lots of colors! When I was brand-new at motherhood I put books on a shelf right above my son's crib, to create a comfortable environment in which books played an important part. As an adult, Joshua is a book lover and avid reader.
- How about creating your very own reading hour with a child? Read from an assortment of books once a week, every other week, or when the time presents itself. Rock the child on your lap and sing a song or two!
- A safe stuffed animal. Check with mom first, though. The child may be "stuffed" with these toys, already.
- A rag doll.
- "Baby." That's what we called the big, floppy doll our son treasured for years. It had a zipper, a belt buckle, a few buttons, and shoelaces. "Baby" was treated as one of the family.
- "Cozy". That's what we called our son's small blanket. Like Linus in the Peanuts cartoon, Josh went everywhere with "Cozy." It looked like a big tattered old Kleenex when we finally retired it from service.
- A pail and shovel. If you want to be extravagant, give him an instant beach. Fill a children's plastic pool with sand.
- Winnie the Pooh sunshade for car window.

Young Children—Clothes

Function is the fashion statement here. Not only are young children beginning to dress themselves, they dress for battle. It would be nice if labels declared ratings for serious play, major grime, and the amount of wear and tear the clothing can bear.

- Look for durability: young children are tough on clothes. They are also growing. If possible, get something that will grow with the child and still make a fashion statement after little Beth sprouts through her bedroom ceiling.
- New sneakers. The faster the better.
- Warm tights for little girls.
- A clip-on tie and a new shirt for a boy.
- Warm snowboots to use while the other pair is drying.
- Pullover sweaters that aren't too bulky.
- A terry cloth bathrobe.

Young Children—Other Things

- Rubber stamps and stamp pads.
- A kitten or puppy. Check with parents first!
- A plastic jump-rope.
- A harmonica. Who cares if it's noisy? The awful silence will come soon enough.
- Chunks of wood from a carpenter. Sand the edges and make a building set. If you are ambitious you could paint or stencil each piece or write the letters of the alphabet.
- Small versions of big tools: hammer, tape measure, screwdriver.
- Books. Find an author who writes for young, new readers. Another book from the child's very first favorite author makes a terrific repeat present.

- Small versions of footballs and basketballs. The Nerf basketball and indoor hoop was a definite winner in our house.
- A piggy bank.
- Write to Dover Publications for their catalogue of activity books for children: 31 East 2nd Street, Mineola, NY 11501.
- Most of the popular children's theme movies have lots of merchandise to offer. If the child has a favorite movie, look for a theme toy or article. Josh still has his collection of Star Wars figures from twenty years ago. It is tucked away for sentimental (and investment!) reasons.
- Make homemade gift certificates and take the lucky child on a "Queen or King for a Day" shopping spree (especially the week after Christmas when bargains abound). Include a coupon for a sundae at the ice cream store.
- Give gift certificates from fast-food restaurants or ice cream stores.
- Children delight in videos. If you have a severe budget restraint, check with video rental stores to see if they will be retiring any—and pick them up for a song.
- Call a plumber and ask if he knows where you could get leftover pieces of PVC pipe and some fittings. A little sandpaper on the rough edges and shazam! The world's biggest building set!
- Look for a perfectly good bicycle at a thrift store. Paint it with the child. Go crazy.
- Children's beginner ski sets appear at thrift stores every year after Thanksgiving. So do ice skates. Watch for them.
- Buy polished rocks. Fill up a pint Mason jar. Decorate the rim with ribbon. Magic.

- Does the child have a favorite cereal? Buy a couple of boxes and wrap with red ribbon.
- What would be more fun than a pretty box lined with a piece of velvet? Get one and fill it with colorful costume jewelry.
- Invest in a sketch pad at a discount store. Include a package of pastel chalk or colored pencils. Write a project idea on each page such as: draw your house, paint a picture of your favorite day, mix and create colors by designing a quilt.
- Order a subscription to a magazine written especially for children.
- Buy a nifty new lunch box.
- Educational software.
- A battery-powered toothbrush.
- Take the child to tea.

A Tip From Laura: Laura is my young friend. She is also an expert in the young child department since she recently was a young child herself and has two brothers who still are. What was her immediate response to the question, "What is the best gift in the whole, wide, world?" Get ready for this—a dump truck of dirt. Laura's mom could only nod her head and sigh in agreement. Laura and her brothers spent the entire summer turning a hill of dirt into flat space. They burrowed, tunneled, built, tumbled, slid, imagined, jumped, rolled, sculpted, raced, traveled, and had a gay old time on their pile of dirt. Come to think of it, I spent a good deal of time tumbling and sliding on a dirt hill once, too. Maybe you can get creative about this. (See why you need durable clothes?)

Pre-Teens—Clothes

Juniors are starting to become fashion conscious. As much as we scream against them, there *are* clothing trends, and we ourselves have tried a few. (Remember that madras blouse you couldn't live without?) If you want to know what's in, go to a children's store or pay attention to what other kids are wearing. You will soon see similarities, either in shoes, clothing or hairstyles. Keep one thing in mind: there is nothing *worse* for a child than to get something that was popular before, but isn't now. To figure out fashion in the pre-teen department, you would do well to enlist the help of a (listen to me) *young* store clerk. Don't go to the grandmother-types: they will be too sensible.

- Hair gadgets for girls and baseball caps for boys.
- Sweatshirts emblazoned with a popular logo.
- Stylish pocketbook.
- Stylish bathing suits—please keep modesty in mind!
- Ski parka.
- Belts—but, please! Not the kind grandpa wears!
- Shirt and tie.
- Colorful vests for girls.
- Sandals or water shoes.
- Sweat set.
- Terry cloth bathrobe.

Pre-Teens—Other Things

- "Cool" sunglasses.
- Wallets.
- An all-in-one disposable camera, along with a photo album.
- Music tapes or CDs of a favorite group.

- Subscription to a magazine written just for this age group.
- A day of adventure: why not take your nephew to an amusement park or play miniature golf with a niece on her birthday?
- Certificates for free pizza.
- A small flashlight.
- An all-in-one tool, like a Swiss Army knife.
- Something that will last a lifetime: a quality recipe box. When I gave these to Olivia and Leah for Christmas last year, I adorned the package with a good set of measuring spoons. I expect those two to stuff those boxes with treasures (hopefully of the recipe variety!) and still use them when they are old.
- It would be a great gift to teach a young teen a skill: I *should* spend some time in the kitchen showing Olivia and Leah how to use those spoons! Take a youngster along for companionship when you fish, change the oil in your car, shop for groceries. Teach as you go.
- Get some educational software.
- Books written with children this age in mind. Detective series are very popular.
- A sketch book with a box of pastels or colored pencils.
- A diary.

Teens—Clothes

Unless you are certain about your clothing purchase, I heartily recommend a gift certificate to a favorite clothing store for your teen friend. Shoes and clothes are critically important in defining "the look" that each teen strives for. It will be a waste of your money if you are uninformed—or worse—too practical.

Teens—Other Things

- Pretty things for the bathroom: bubble bath, bath oil in a pretty jar sealed with wax.
- Stationery.
- Blank journals.
- A teen Bible or daily devotional or flip calendar.
- Subscriptions for magazines written just for teens … or fashion magazines written for the general public. A subscription to a magazine that deals in a particular area of interest might be appreciated, also. For instance, does the teen own a horse? How about *Horse Illustrated*?
- A personal telephone. (Check with Mom or Dad if you're not the teen's parent.)
- Makeup pouches with an assortment of makeup brushes.
- Hair brushes and combs.
- After-shave, cologne, or perfume.
- Soft-sided duffel bag designed for books, gym equipment, clothes.
- Books.
- Tickets to a concert.
- Tapes or CDs of favorite musicians.
- Take the teen to dinner—just the two of you. Get all dressed up.
- A key chain (for the car keys, of course!).
- A watch.
- Jewelry.
- A camera.
- A day planner.
- A pen and pencil set.

6

Uh-Oh, What Do I Get Now?
THE HARD-TO-BUY-FOR CROWD

"Don't Get Me Anything!"—Seniors

I think it takes all the grace and tact that come from living seventy, eighty, ninety years, for seniors to get through yet another onslaught of gadgets, knickknacks, and otherwise useless junk that clutters their homes when a holiday or birthday comes along. When Grandma growls, "You shouldn't have," through gritted teeth, she probably means it.

I've spoken to dozens of senior citizens and to a person, they say the same thing: "Most of us don't *need* anything. We don't *want* more clutter—we want to get *rid* of clutter!"

What to do? First, listen to what people say. If they say they really don't want more *stuff*, honor that request. Tough to do, isn't it, when this is one category of people we want to honor by giving gifts? Don't worry; there are some helpful suggestions in this chapter.

One special note: some of our elderly *are* in need. Pay attention. Assess individual situations. Some might need money, or food, or a ride to the doctor a whole lot more than a glow-in-the-dark bubble light.

Give the Gift of Friendship

- Many seniors are lonely. Pay a visit. But, please, don't start something that you will not continue. If you intend to visit regularly, do so. Let me share a sorrowful story about an old man named John: Years and years ago, I mentioned to John that I was going to haul a carload of little kids trick-or-treating. This was deep in mountainous back country. I thought about going to John's cabin, but decided against stopping since after all, he was an old bachelor off in the woods. I felt awful later when he told me he drove to a far away store for sweets and stayed up late with the lantern on. We never knocked on his door. John was hurt, and I learned a painful lesson at his expense.

- While you are visiting, wash a window, sweep a floor, do the dishes.

- The elderly are fearful of becoming a burden or nuisance to others. Many need rides to town, to the doctor, to church. Pay attention. And take a senior for a ride in the countryside just for fun. Stop for ice cream.

- Take an older person to lunch or breakfast. Dinner fare is often too heavy and late nights upset routine. Get all dressed up. Go someplace ritzy, where lunch is affordable.

- Go for a walk in the park together. Don't be in a hurry. My mom would think it a gift if I was able to spend time with her without having to run off to my next appointment.

- Ask an older person to teach you a particular skill. It might be crochet or carpentry. You will learn something new, and honor the other person in a mighty way.

- Do an elderly person's laundry.

Seniors—Other Things

- Nostalgic items are popular. *If the person has a tape player,* purchase old-time radio shows or a tape of Big Band music. Subscribe to a magazine called *Reminisce* on that person's behalf. Their address is: P.O. Box 572, Milwaukee, WI 53201-0572.

- If the person enjoys a particular hobby or collection, you have a vast gift opportunity.

- Give gift certificates to someplace a bit out of the ordinary. How about for a caramel sundae at the local soda shop? Seniors, if not diabetic, love sweets.

- A night-light or a lightweight easy-to-use flashlight.

- A daily "flip" devotional calendar.

- A subscription to *Reader's Digest*. If eyesight is poor, large print editions can be ordered. Their address is: Pleasantville, NY 10570.

- Perfume or talcum powder, *if* they don't already have a dresser full!

- Hankies for men.

- A bolo tie. Regular business ties are not essential at this age, but some men like to wear string ties when they are dressing up.

- A belt buckle with the man's initials.

- Fruit baskets.

- Nuts.

- Hard candies with wrappers. If the person is diabetic, find sugar-free candies.

- An African violet or a small plant if you think it would be appreciated.

- A music box.
- Playing cards, if applicable. Older friends, Grace and Jim, play a children's card game called "SkipBo" by the hour.
- Gift certificates to a clothing store, so they can buy what they need—or like. Some of us want to stuff our elderly into the latest fashion craze—much to their chagrin and discomfort!
- A wraparound bathrobe that ties in front or has Velcro. Depending on age, reconsider anything you are buying that has buttons—tough on arthritic fingers.
- A box of stationery with a supply of self-stick postage stamps.
- A lap robe.
- A one- or two-person crockpot, or an electric teakettle.
- Word find or crossword workbooks with large print.
- Does your senior friend miss someone special who is far, far away? Give the gift of a long-distance phone call. Just have the call charged to your calling card number. For seniors on fixed income, a *long*, long-distance phone call to a friend would be a thrill.

Put Lots of Thought into This

For some elderly people, a pet would make a good gift *if* you are not creating work or aggravation for the person: animals, even if they swim in a small bowl, require care. They also provide unconditional love and constant companionship, protection, and in some cases, aid. For a person who is hearing impaired, a small dog might fit the bill, but consider everything before you present a pet:

Where will the pet relieve itself? Who will clean the pet's waste? Are there ordinances, covenants, or neighbors that must be considered? Will the animal get exercise? Who will bring the pet to the vet? Is the person allergic to animals? Would the person appreciate having an animal companion? Can the person afford care and food? If the person travels (i.e. goes south each winter), can the pet go, too?

If you decide that this is a good gift in spite of all the possible problems, do try to find an older animal that is already trained and mellow. Don't think that all animals at the pound are problem pets. There are many reasons why people have to give up their pets. We have had a few critters from the pound who were perfect in every way.

No Cost, but Great Rewards!

My sister Sheila practically trembled at the thought of peeking into her overgrown garden. Two years of neglect left it in terrible disrepair—and Sheila in despair. While she rolled up her sleeves and went to work weeding, she thought of the small community of Russian immigrants in her town who had escaped religious persecution in Russia. They were all old. Sheila and her husband befriended them and often invited them to their home. Years ago she had promised they could have a garden on her land. She made a sheepish call. Soon, a battalion of Babushkas appeared with rakes in hand. They were beaming so broadly their faces almost split; cooped up in small city apartments, they had no chance to feel and work the earth. The garden is immaculate now. It's been planted with seeds Sheila supplied. Sheila's gift of space is one that sings in the hearts of those Russian women.

Four-Star Gift Idea

This will take some planning and super-sleuth work on your part, so start early. Make a "This Is Your Life" video of an older person's life journey, complete with music and narration. Begin at the home or hospital where he or she was born. Continue on through the different homes, find the playground, the school, the church attended. Work your way up through life, as best you can. Include interviews with people. What a testimony! What a gift!

Nursing Homes

- Please visit. Let me say that again. *Please visit.* And bring your children with you. Bring your *pet,* if allowed. I once borrowed a baby goat and brought it to an old man who sat in stony silence in his wheelchair. Without a sound, his big paw of a hand rested on the head of that animal as tears filled his eyes.

- If the person can read, purchase a subscription to the hometown newspaper.

- A cork board with a few colorful tacks to pin up pictures or mementos. Get tacks with big thick ends for ease in handling.

- An occasional spray of flowers *if* appreciated. To some who are tucked away in nursing homes, flowers are a reminder of death. Be sensitive.

- A flower or tree that can be planted outside of the nursing home, most especially within viewing range from where the person regularly sits. Plant it in the person's honor. Hang a homemade plaque from a branch.

- Send a supply of wrapped candies that the person can hand out to staff or visiting children.
- Sweatpants, or a sweatshirt that closes in front.
- Slipper socks with non-skid soles.
- An outing, *if* you are capable of accepting the responsibility and able to meet the requirements of the person. Needless to say, all of these suggestions depend on the person's ability to cope physically and mentally.

The Mentally Challenged

Jim and Karen and I visited for some time in the back room of a thrift shop that is run on behalf of the developmentally disabled in our community. My years of trading at this shop have softened the edge on my uncertainty around these dear people; I've had the opportunity to learn there is nothing to be afraid of. As a matter of fact, I had the opportunity to learn that people who are disabled—physically and mentally—are among the *happiest* people in our society!

Jim and Karen know this, and emphatically stated that it is our "loss" if we do not know people who are challenged. For those of us who *do* know them, *what to get them* can be a challenge!

- Try to get something that will help with dexterity and focus. Karen reached up on a shelf and pulled down a children's game called "Perfection." "Something like this is perfect," she said, pointing to all the intricate shapes and designs in the game. You will always have to take the person's level of disability into consideration, but be willing to try things— sometimes capabilities are far above what we might expect.

- Present your friend with a set of used golf clubs. They needn't be complete. Paint the balls orange or bright yellow if the person has vision problems.
- Give a gift of makeup. Take the time to teach application.
- When you purchase clothing, try to find things that are easy to put on and fasten. Also, avoid white because of potential food stains, and buy things that are washable and do not need ironing.
- Try to stay clear of laces if buying anything that ties. Get Velcro.
- Costume jewelry is a big hit. So are watches. Be certain the person is not allergic to metal.
- A sensible lunch kit if the person works. There are soft-sided kits out now that maintain foods at cold or warm temperatures.
- Coloring books and crayons.
- If the person is intrigued by music, scout around for an old guitar. Or buy a new harmonica.
- Jigsaw puzzles.
- This was a puzzle to me—word find books! Karen and Jim say that even though there is little to no understanding of word meanings, the words are found indeed. These books keep mentally challenged friends occupied for hours!
- A fake microphone.
- M & M's.
- Coffee, if someone keeps an apartment, and if there is no dietary restriction.
- Personalized labels to put on their things. It gives them ownership.

- A photograph of the person—in a special frame. A sure winner!
- Backpacks or duffel bags.
- An outing, most especially to a restaurant.
- And the bestest gift of all: a hug and an in-your-eye smile!

The Sight-Impaired

- A telephone call. A blind person cannot doodle or fuss with things when on the phone; they are all yours when you call. A phone call is a chance to connect with other people, and is highly prized by the sight-impaired.
- Audio tapes of books, magazines, radio shows.
- A manicure or pedicure.
- An offer to take someone shopping. From time to time I take my sight-impaired friend to a store (like the kitchen gadget shop) and walk her through the aisles, explaining nearly every display and product. I put things in her hands so she can evaluate through feel.
- Read to the person. I visit that same friend every few weeks and read my latest (sigh) attempts at the "great American novel." She happily points out my split infinitives!
- A comfortable "throw" with a distinguishable texture for when the person wants a light blanket for a nap.
- A talking clock.
- Become a personal secretary—write letters, pay bills.
- Become a personal valet—help with wardrobe, colors, hair design.

The American Foundation for the Blind

For help for the visually impaired, contact this group at: 15 W 16th Street, New York, NY 10011, (800) 232-5463.

The Hearing-Impaired

- Find an interpreter to accompany the person to a performance or family event.
- *Learn to sign* yourself. You can attend a class or learn on your computer.
- Captioned videos.
- TV set with a decoder built in that decodes closed-caption for video or broadcast.
- Signed story videotapes—a delight for youngsters!
- Flashing or vibrating alarm clock, doorbell, smoke alarm, phone (for those who have an amplifier on the phone).
- Telephone earphones for those who are partially impaired.
- Books, magazines, and word-puzzle workbooks.
- For parents: a flashing baby monitor.
- A Telecommunications Device for the phone *as well* as one for a close relative who is not impaired so communication is possible.

National Information Center on Deafness

The NICD is a centralized source of information about hearing loss and deafness. It collects, develops, and disseminates up-to-date information on deafness, hearing loss, and the organizations and services for people who are deaf and hard-of-hearing. Contact them for a vast selection of catalogs to aid you in finding a helpful gift for your hearing-impaired friend at: NICD, Gallaudet University, 800 Florida Avenue NE, Washington, DC 20002, (202) 651-5051.

The Chair-Bound

- Sheepskin products designed for comforting a chair-bound person.
- Gloves.
- Remote-control operated appliances: TV, VCR, lights.
- A "reach" stick.
- A trip someplace usually not accessible and spectacularly beautiful—you provide the brawn or brains to make the outing possible.
- A shopping trip, especially for groceries that are too high or too low to reach.
- Create a "garden" spot in the backyard and build a ramp; hang a bird feeder down low, raise flower beds up high.
- Lap robe.
- A promise to meet and play cards once a week.

National Library Services for the Handicapped

This is a network of fifty-six regional and over one hundred local libraries that provide free library service in both audio and Braille, as well as help for the physically handicapped. Contact them at 1291 Taylor Street NW, Washington, DC 20542, (800) 424-8567.

Disabled American Veterans

This fine organization offers help for the handicapped. Contact them at P.O. Box 14301, Cincinnati, OH 45250, (606) 441-7300.

For the One Who Really Has It All

What now? I mean, this guy already has *everything*. *Two* of everything! Not to mention that his preferences run to the persnickety! But he's a pretty nice guy, and you want to get him a gift that means something. Three things come to mind: charity, food, and adventure.

Charity

Perform a civic duty or serve as a volunteer at the person's favorite charity or cause. Suppose the person is an animal lover? Donate your services to the Humane Society or the local pound and do so in your friend's name. If the person has a heart for the poor, stir the stew pot at a shelter and serve the needy. If he's an environmentalist, rake and clean a dirty city lot. You get the idea.

Food

I have one friend who could be the poster child for the has-everything crowd! Whenever I am at his home I throw together a loaf of bread while we are chatting.

Unless someone can't eat chocolate (I didn't say "like"—there is no such thing as someone who doesn't *like* chocolate!), make a batch of brownies—or chocolate chip cookies.

Adventure

Your friend might have everything, but I bet he hasn't *done* everything! Go to the chamber of commerce in your town and study the pamphlets. Find an adventure, then spring for tickets. It might be as low-key as sitting on a lawn listening to bluegrass (adventure comes in fending off mosquitoes), or as thrilling as an afternoon on a white-water raft.

And One More Idea

This might be a perfect gift for a member of the has-everything crowd. Show up at the person's home, camera in hand. Throughout the day take candid shots of the person at rest, at work, at play. Make sure you get outside and inside pictures of the home. Look for interesting features. Include pets, cars, boats, even neighbors! Once developed, paste the pictures in a small, spiral picture album (found at photo and print shops), and print *"A Day in the Life of_____."*

7

Just Heavenly
EXPRESSIVE GIFTS FOR
RELIGIOUS OCCASIONS

Many events in a person's life are connected to the spiritual: baptism, communion, confirmation, Bar/Bat Mitzvah, and weddings, to name a few. These are most often celebrations to which friends and family are invited, and to which we customarily bring gifts. This chapter looks at our most common religious activities and offers suggestions. Your gift need not come from one of these lists. You may choose to give something suggested elsewhere in this book, for example, something from the infants' and children's chapter.

Baptism or Dedication—Child or Infant
- Christening robe with initials.
- White blanket, perhaps adorned with lace.
- White beeswax candle.
- Religious wall plaque.
- Engraved Bible. How about a "Baby Bible" that incorporates a section in which to record the child's church record?
- Bible storybooks, music, or videos.
- Cross.

- Jewelry with religious symbolism.
- White sweater.
- Booties.
- Bonnet.
- Picture of a child with Jesus, or of a guardian angel.
- Name plaque.

Baptism—Adult

- Engraved Bible.
- Engraved prayer book or devotional; a book on prayer.
- Book of daily meditations.
- Special bookmark.
- Picture or wall plaque.
- Inspirational music tape.
- A ride to church or Bible study.
- If you are knowledgeable, some time spent in discipling the individual.
- An easy-to-read book on theology.
- Necklace with cross.
- A hearty welcome.

Bris or Naming Ceremony

A Bris is a ceremonial circumcision performed on Jewish baby boys at home shortly after birth. Jewish baby girls have naming ceremonies.

- Any sort of religious artifact that will help the child develop religious identity.
- A silver Kiddush cup.
- A mezuzah.

- A necklace with the Jewish symbol for life (chai).
- A plaque showing the meaning of the child's Hebrew name.
- A tree planted in Israel. Contact: Jewish National Fund, 42 East 69th Street, New York, NY 10021, (800) 542-8733.

Note: It is customary to present the parents of a firstborn son with five silver dollars when the child is one month old. The parents are to "use" this money to buy the child back from God.

First Communion/Confirmation

- Bible.
- Prayer book.
- White gloves, sweater, or shawl.
- Veil for girls, white tie for boys.
- Children's devotional; may I suggest *My Utmost for His Highest* by Oswald Chambers for an older child.
- A piece of engraved jewelry.
- Flowers.
- Special bookmark.
- Pen and pencil set.
- Bible cover, carrying case, highlighter.
- Money or savings bond.
- Watch.

Bar/Bat Mitzvah

This is akin to a "coming of age." For a Jewish girl, it is usually celebrated at age twelve, for a boy, age thirteen. This ceremony has profound cultural and spiritual meaning, and is reason for great celebration.

- The symbol for chai (life) in the Jewish language also represents the number eighteen. Consequently, it is a custom to give money in increments of eighteen dollars to the Bat or Bar Mitzvah. For a very special relative or friend, you could give ten chais, or $180. Any number of chais is appropriate.
- A tallis (for boys), tallis clips (for prayer shawl).
- A Haggadah (Passover prayer book).
- Jewish religious artifacts.
- A menorah (candleholder for Chanukah).
- A Jewish book, such as *Wisdom of Israel* or *Folklore of Jewish People*.
- Savings bonds.
- Jewish Bible or Torah.
- Embroidered velvet case to hold prayer book, prayer shawl.
- Shabbat candlesticks (for girl).
- Kiddush cup (wine cup).
- Seder plate and/or matzo holder (for Passover).
- Custom-embroidered yarmulke (skullcap).
- Star of David print, or jewelry.

*For a wonderful selection of gifts, write for a catalogue: Hamakor Judaica, Inc., P.O. Box 48836, Niles, IL 60714-0836, (708) 966-4040.

Weddings

Probably the three main reasons to give a gift are birthdays, Christmas, and weddings. These three events vie for top honors as "budget thumper of the year." If you have a particularly full plate of spring weddings, you may want to spring for something nice, but affordable. It can be done!

Engagement

If you are inclined to give a gift for a couple's engagement, consider a good wedding planner, or books on weddings. A gift subscription to a wedding magazine is a good idea, too. A touching gift from a professional friend for Josh and Molly was several sessions of premarital counseling.

If the couple is low on funds, send them a copy of *You Can Afford the Wedding of Your Dreams.**

Showers

Quite often, the person hosting a wedding shower will inform you of a particular "theme." It may be kitchen, bath, lingerie, and so on. This makes picking a gift a bit easier because it defines an area of interest. Shower presents usually run toward setting up the home and augmenting the trousseau. It is not uncommon to give your practical gift at the wedding shower, and cash for the wedding.

Low-Cost, but Delightful Wedding or Shower Gifts

It is highly probable that the bride and groom have registered at a few favorite stores. Registries are convenient and sensible. If you are on a limited income, try to get to the stores quickly so you will have a good selection of items within your price range. But don't panic if you can't afford the items selected—just buy something else.

Remember, this is a *gift*, not an ultimatum. I know we have managed to turn this into obligation and duty. We act as though we have pledged to drive ourselves mad and flirt with

*Servant Publications

the poorhouse over this business of gift-giving. But that's poppycock. Put thought, sincerity, and pizazz in your gift and go home and put up your feet.

- Make your specialty bread, brownies, cookies, or cake. Buy a shiny new pan, include some fancy ingredients, the recipe, stick the whole thing in a basket and decorate the handle with cookie cutters or a tiny rolling pin. If vanilla is an ingredient, buy a bottle of the real stuff. Chocolate? Go to a specialty shop and buy a small package of "designer" cocoa powder.

- Visit an antiques mall and find two lovely china tea cups and saucers. Add a small plate for crumpets. Tell the couple that these are *just for the two of them*. Joe and I have special teacups. When one of us takes them down from the shelf, we know we are going to have a gentle, private moment between the two of us.

- *Love for a Lifetime* by James Dobson.

- Couple's devotional Bible.

- An afghan. It would be wonderful if you made it yourself and if it matched their couch.

- A healthy houseplant.

- Collect as many interesting, small old jars as you can. Wash them squeaky clean. Go to a bulk food store and fill each with an herb or spice. Put care in crafting labels for each jar. Present them in a basket. If you want to splurge you could find a paperback book on cooking with spices.

- Purchase two pasta bowls, which are usually wide. Put in a package of specialty pasta and a spaghetti ladle. Add a tiny bottle of imported olive oil or a cheese grater if you like. If you can wrap this as a bundle in a red-and-white-checked tablecloth, bravo!

- An old bowl in good condition is an excellent wedding gift. Some antique stores sell these things for as little as $20. Use your imagination when presenting it.
- A basket filled with handy home gadgets—could be for kitchen, bath, or garage. Think ahead to when the new couple will be hanging curtain rods, pictures, and will be needing a piece of twine or package of tape.
- Give an ingredient (rice would be nice since it's a wedding) and provide a list of "Ten Things to Do" with the ingredient.
- Books that help with the practical matters of life. Consider a book on how to fix things or do simple carpentry, electrical, and plumbing repairs. For example, s*ensible cookbooks,* not the ones requiring the acumen of a master chef and with impractical recipes. A book on money management, frugal living, *gift-giving*, and decorating. Get a copy of my other book, *1001 Bright Ideas to Stretch Your Dollars*, Servant Publications. (See page at the end of the book for more information.)
- Are you a needlepoint person? Frame something apropos.
- A beautiful flowerpot or a pretty flower vase. Know what I'd do? I'd give a simple but attractive flower vase and then a few gift certificates for bouquets of cut flowers from the local supermarket.
- Pictures YOU took at the wedding or reception that would have special meaning. Frame them nicely.

- A board game. Note I said board, not "bored." Get something fun. Scrabble is a sure winner.
- An iron, along with a gift certificate to a local cleaner so the couple can have their pressing done for the first month. You could say something silly like, "Iron you smart?"
- A wooden recipe box that looks as if it will withstand the test of time—fill it with kitchen tips and favorite recipes.
- How about my money-saving, idea-packed newsletter: To subscribe write to *Friendly Advice: Frugal Living With Style*. The mailing address is: Friendly Advice, Box 13, Bigfork, MT 59911.

Give the Gift of Yourself

If you have a particular skill, offer it to the couple as a gift. They might need you.

- Are you good with a camera? Offer to take photos at the wedding, reception, or showers to augment what the professional photographer is doing. (People hide when I enter a room with a camera.)
- Can you bake? Your skills may be needed and you may be up to your elbows in dinner rolls, Italian cookies, or Polish Babka bread before you know it.
- Can you decorate a cake *very well*? Offer the wedding cake as your gift.
- Can you decorate a space well? We attended a wedding reception recently that was held in a community hall. A woman borrowed good wicker furniture from everyone in town and filled the space with the furniture, a trellis, an arbor, and fountains. Potted plants were stuffed into every nook and cranny.

- Do you *grow* pretty flowers? Can you arrange them?
- Can you arrange food on a buffet table with flair?
- Are you good at calligraphy? Offer your skill and print announcements, thank-you cards, place cards.
- Do you have a classic vehicle or horse and carriage the couple would be thrilled to ride in after the wedding? Offer it as your gift.
- Can you sew? There are endless possibilities.
- Can you sing or play an instrument? (Come on, now … I mean, can you *really* sing?)
- Are you a profoundly ordered person? Offer your services to organize the wedding party at the church.
- Do you have a beautiful yard, garden, meadow, home where the wedding could be held?
- If young children are involved, are you a terrific baby-sitter?
- Can you offer to videotape the wedding?
- Can you offer to serve food at the wedding as your gift?
- Can you offer to clean up—or *return* all that borrowed wicker? MAJOR gift!

Other Wedding Gifts

- Money. The groom will love you forever.
- Savings bond.
- Specific help with the honeymoon plans. Can you loan a vehicle, a vacation condo, participate in the cost?
- One of Josh and Molly's best gifts was having their two close friends flown to the wedding as a gift from a dear couple who share a big heart.
- A place setting of china.

- Flatware or silver setting.
- Crystal.
- Higher-end items on the bridal registry.
- A picture or print, particularly if the picture has sentimental value. Josh and Molly live in Washington, D.C. Josh's high school chums bought him a print of the lake in Montana beside which he grew up. The gift has very special meaning.
- Find a gifted calligrapher and ask that the wedding announcement be elaborately printed and specially framed, or ask the calligrapher to print a special verse that was used during the wedding ceremony.
- A gourmet cooking class for the new couple. How about Italian?
- A good starter tool kit for the groom *and* the bride. Paint hers a pretty color.
- A matching pair of high-quality, white terry cloth bathrobes with hoods. Throw in some massage oil.
- A good quality, non-stick frying pan.
- An espresso machine, if you think it will be used. Don't be too quick with the pasta machine—it may end up sitting on a shelf.
- A big crockpot and a crockpot cookbook.
- Gift certificates for dinner at their favorite restaurant ... after they are married and when they realize how broke they are!
- Camping gear.
- For the Jewish couple: Shabbat candlesticks and candles.
- A positive smash is a box of spices designed specifically as a wedding gift. It's from Penzey's, merchants of quality spices. This is a winner and a thrill to receive, partly because

it is so different. Penzey's has an assortment of gift boxes to choose from, and the cost is from under $20 and up. Write or call for their catalogue. Just be certain to order soon enough to have the gift arrive for the wedding. Penzey's, P.O. Box 1448, Waukesha, WI 53187, (414) 574-0277, FAX (414) 574-0278.

What We Did

We wanted to give our son, Joshua, and his bride, Molly, something special on their wedding day. We set out to find gifts that would be long-lasting, sentimental, significant, and appreciated.

- We searched and searched until we found a good quality pocket watch for our son. A jeweler engraved the back of the watch with "Husband, love your wife as Christ loves the Church."

- We gave our new daughter, Molly, our heart. A jeweler in our town creates a unique heart every year. The income goes to local charities. Our intent is to present Molly with a new heart every year celebrating the anniversary of her marriage to Josh, and to celebrate the joy she has brought to this family.

8

Red-Letter Days for Blue-Ribbon People
CELEBRATING LIFE'S MEMORABLE MOMENTS

All people celebrate different milestones in life, whether a birthday, a graduation, an anniversary, retirement, or even an illness. These milestones are usually recognized with a gift, or a card, to acknowledge the celebration, the accomplishment, or even the sorrow.

Birthdays

Since this book is filled with gift ideas, I encourage you to study its pages till you find a category the birthday celebrant best fits, and then consider the suggestions. A birthday is an important event. Let's think about the celebration.

- In a sense, someone's birthday is the most special day of the year. It is their very own new year, their very own day of remembrance and reconnoitering with past and present. It should be a celebration. I, for one, do not work on my birthday. No one should. If I were President, I'd make it a law.

- With reasons of their own, some people choose not to celebrate birthdays. Perhaps it reminds them of a time of sorrow, perhaps they don't like the attention. If the person is sincere about not celebrating, honor the request.

- A custom-tailored birthday cake, as mentioned in the food section of Chapter Three, is a thoughtful gift—even if it's a gaily decorated muffin.
- Present a special knife to be used for special ceremonies—like cutting your annual birthday muffin.
- Get all friends or family or both to write a tribute to the person, telling what is unique about his or her character or personality. We don't give sincere compliments often enough. This is your chance.
- Learn something, or participate in something just for the birthday celebrant. For instance, when Josh was young, I taught him a Polish song to sing to my mother on her birthday. She listened with delight.
- Since it is a person's very own special day, I like to give things that use the person's name or initials, whenever possible.
- Send the person on a "treasure hunt" to find your gift. Write an assortment of clues.
- For a child, give a gift that encourages a hobby: a model plane, ship, or car to encourage model building, a few stamps or old bottles, baseball cards, buttons, seashells.
- A friend took pictures at my mother's eightieth party. Her gift? A birthday album filled with memories.

Children's Birthdays

You can create your own version of the "Special Day" that we share with nieces Olivia and Leah each year. We send the birthday child a note that is either filled with options, or describes what we have planned. The day begins with breakfast at a nice restaurant. At breakfast we hand over the piggy bank into which we've been squirreling coins throughout the year. We count the money and place 10 percent of the loot in an envelope and designate it for some special service, charity, or ministry: Olivia has chosen the Veterans' Home, Leah the Humane Society. We do fun things with each girl throughout the day: visit radio stations, parks, or stores. We sightsee, picnic, explore. Last year we held a "joint" Special Day and took them both to an old fort in Canada. They are getting older, and we are designing days to fit their growing interests. This year Olivia will attend a rehearsal at our local theater, followed by dinner and a play. We will probably make arrangements for Leah to visit a woman with an extensive doll collection.

Graduation

- Give *money*. Don't even *think* of a savings bond at a time like this!
- If the graduate is going into special training for a skill of some sort, find equipment or literature that deals with the subject.
- If the person has just finished graduate studies or is entering a field of employment, purchase a first set of business cards.
- Give an attaché case or office equipment as it applies.
- Inscribe a plaque with the person's chosen field: it might say something like "The Doctor Is In" or "Realtor" or "Accountant."
- Have a pen and pencil set engraved.
- Choose an alarm clock, a day planner, a watch, an address book.

- Donate your services for a day: haul a high-school grad to the laundromat, the grocer, the carwash, the mechanic, the variety store, the kitchen, the bank. Teach life skills as you go.
- Buy an easy-to-follow cookbook, a camera, luggage, a backpack.
- Find a good leather traveler's wallet, an all-in-one pocket knife, an electric hot pot if the high school grad is headed for college.
- Did I mention money?

Going Away/New Home

- A subscription to the hometown newspaper to follow the person to the new location, *or* a subscription to the paper in the new location.
- A pizza or bucket of chicken delivered to the new address on moving-in day.
- A memento scrapbook of places of interest in the hometown.
- An autograph book of short notes signed by work associates, relatives, and friends from the hometown.
- Keep the person connected to roots by sending some sort of regional cuisine or specialty item from time to time. We send Joshua coffee beans from his favorite roaster in Montana. Molly gets Cajun food mixes from her mom down in New Orleans.
- One thing we've done for our son every time he's changed his address has been to send away for new address tags for his dog.
- A "Bless This House" metal plaque for the front door, or a mezuza for the doorpost in a Jewish home.

- Start a clipping of an outdoor or indoor plant from the hometown. Send it to the new home in a pretty planter. Remember my "Presbyterian ivy" from Pennsylvania?
- A smoke alarm.
- An elaborate door knocker.
- Make a road kit: Fill a basket with road maps, spare change, wrapped snacks, a couple of water bottles, napkins, magic marker, flashlight, a couple of flares.
- An organizer pouch for the sun visor.
- Travel mending kit, or a first aid kit.
- A pen that actually writes when held upside down.
- A book on tape. If it's a long trip, make it two books on tape.
- A big hug.

Anniversary/Romance

Joe always brings me the first wildflower to bloom on our property. It is called a "Shooting Star." Every year, my husband walks into the house and offers this token of his love. His gift is simple, spontaneous, and free, yet it tells me that he thought of me, and that's the greatest gift of all.

- Plant a tree. We planted a Ponderosa pine in honor of our son's wedding. We call it the "Jolly-Mosh" tree!
- Present your mate with a homemade coupon book. Include such things as a foot bath, back rub, car wash, banana split, candlelight dinner, or an "I give in—you're right!" coupon. Use your imagination. Would your wife know you loved her if you really (I mean *really*) showed interest while shopping with her? Would your husband fall over in shock if you plopped down with a bowl of popcorn in front of the TV to

watch Monday Night Football? Certificates can also be used to say you're sorry.

- Give jewelry. How about a locket or a cameo?
- Present her with perfume or cologne.
- Buy lingerie. (Most *wives* would fall over in shock if their husband brought home something lacy for them!)
- Take a course together. Learn Chinese cooking.
- Go to a bed and breakfast or a charming inn, just for the night.
- Pack a picnic basket for two.
- Tie up a bundle of scented potpourri in an old lace hankie. Or make "tea-potpourri" with aromatic herbal tea bags. Use a pretty ribbon to tie.
- Create a "day of the month" for gift-giving.
- Find candlesticks. Then use them.
- Search for the perfect music box.
- Even though we aren't Jewish, I plan to surprise Joe with a mezuza (doorpost ornament) that bears the inscription "Ani L'Dodi," which is the Hebrew quotation for "I am my beloved's and my beloved is mine." It will be perfect for the "Isle of View" sack. (See "Romantic Gifts" in Chapter Three.)

Illness

- Of course, the standby, flowers. But just a note: *sometimes* these things are a nuisance and create nothing but aggravation for the caregiver who has to figure out how to get everything either home from the hospital, or arrange them at home so they don't get in the way. We've reached a point that we think we have to send flowers if someone is ill. Not necessarily. I will sometimes bring a *small*, single bud vase as my flower. With the proper presentation (I don't just stick a flower in a vase without greens, or ribbon), this serves its purpose well.
- Consider a plant that will last, rather than flowers, *if* you are not creating the additional burden of caring for the plant.
- Easy-to-read books or magazines.
- My friend Jo makes a point of sending a cooked dinner to the home of someone who is too ill (or too busy caring for someone ill) to cook for the family.
- Does someone's garden need tending, pets or livestock need caring for, house need cleaning, clothes need ironing? Do it.
- Does someone need a ride to the doctor, or to make a daily visit to the hospital or nursing home? Take him.
- Sheepskin-covered hot water bottle.
- Afghan or throw.
- Warm, non-skid slippers.
- An electric razor.
- A lightweight but warm robe that ties in front.
- A scalp or hand massage if the person is agreeable.
- A book on tape.
- A *short* visit.

- A colorful helium balloon.
- For a child: a safe, small stuffed animal or a doll. I'd wager an adult would enjoy a cuddly little critter, too!
- Chicken soup.

Retirement

- Tickets to a vast assortment of regional events.
- A trip.
- A short-wave radio.
- A weather radio.
- Golf clubs (not necessarily the entire set).
- Membership (short- or long- term) to a health club or spa.
- A massage.
- A full make-over at a spa or a beauty shop.
- Fishing gear.
- A memorial tree planted on the grounds of employment.
- Pay tuition for some sort of course: woodworking, cooking, becoming an amateur naturalist.
- A camera.
- Binoculars and a book on bird watching.
- An illustrated book on gardening.

Funerals/Death

- There is no other time when a gift of your service might be more appreciated. For instance, can you make phone calls to inform others of the death and arrangements? Offer to help the survivor make arrangements.
- Just show up and do the laundry, or polish shoes, or dust the house.

- Food is usually a most welcome gift right now. You may volunteer your organizational skills to take care of perishables, marking bowls for proper return.
- Memorials are often mentioned in the obituary. If no requests are made, donate to an interest group, hospice, or a local volunteer group in memory of the deceased.
- Money could be a very needed and appreciated gift right now. Don't think your few dollars will not count: perhaps a relative needs gas money just to drive to the funeral. Between phone calls and final arrangements, not to mention costly medical bills, this is when every penny counts.
- A book of poetry.
- Flowers—fresh cut or to plant in memory of the deceased.
- An inspirational book to help the survivor cope.
- A visit. Jewish people "sit Shiva" for one week, during which time people gather at the home and visit the surviving family. It is positively taboo for the bereaved to cook food or serve themselves during this week.
- One of the best gifts you can give is not forgetting. After several weeks, the shock of the death wears off some, and survivors can find themselves mighty lonely, especially if it is the remaining marriage partner who faces life alone. A call, a visit, a card or letter, or an invitation to dinner would be a meaningful gift. Let the survivor talk and talk and talk about the loved one. Such conversation is healing.

9

Ho Ho Ho—A-Gifting We Will Go
THE HAPPY HOLIDAYS

Now it is time to turn our attention to specific holidays, as tradition puts us in the *what to give, what to bring* state of mind. Thus far, the pages of this book have been jammed with ideas, and the final chapter gives hundreds of suggestions for giving to those with specific occupations, sports, or interests. Most holidays, however, do come with definite gift applications, and we will address them in this chapter.

New Year's Day, January 1

This is not necessarily a gift-giving occasion. By the New Year, with the glut of Christmas behind them, people are turning attention towards personal improvement and resolutions. (We call them "revolutions" in our house.) Some regional customs prevail, but they apply more to meal preparation than to presents. Some suggestions, however are:

- Calendars. Humorous or inspirational flip calendars are popular.
- Day planners.
- Calorie counting charts.

- Anything to do with exercise—small hand weights, sweatbands, athletic socks, and so forth.
- Journals or diaries.
- A garden plan book.
- A current best-selling novel.
- A vegetarian cookbook.
- Earmuffs (for the resolute new walker in the family).
- New big-handled toothbrush and floss. (I'm convinced the number one New Year's resolution is to floss.)
- A big jar of honey.

Valentine's Day, February 14

This is one day you don't want to miss! It is meant for lovers, but everyone—grandma, the children, the teacher—enjoys the special day. It's a pretty easy holiday as far as gifts go, because people tend to expect the customary fare:

- Candy! It perturbs me that Valentine's Day comes so close behind New Year's Day, the day I decide to banish fat from my life forever. Poor Joe gets mixed signals from me every year. Yes, get me candy, no, don't you dare! Go ahead! DARE! Nothing beats a heart-shaped box filled with sweets.
- Hearts! Remember our collection of hearts on the bedroom wall? Start one yourself. And what is better than giving *your* heart? Adopt a pet. Become a Big Brother or Big Sister. Visit a hospital with a fistful of … something!
- Flowers! Order in advance, though, because florists are swamped for the occasion. You could also purchase a lovely spray of cut flowers at the local supermarket, or find an attractive silk flower arrangement in a gift shop or at a major discounter.

- Cupids! Or other little knickknacks that bring a message of love. Fifteen years ago Joe presented me with a little plastic dog holding a heart in his mouth that says "Be Mine." That little dog is barely more than an inch high, but it is a treasure that sits looking up at me right this minute. Many gift shops carry whimsical statues of angels—a lovely gift for someone you love.
- Birds! Not just figurines. If you've weighed all the responsibilities, how about a canary or a parakeet? Time was, just about every grandma and grandpa I knew had a bird.
- Nuts! *Nuts?* Sure! I've made this many times: line a heart-shaped tin with foil and butter the foil well.

COCO-NUT HEART

Recipe: Melt 1/3 cup butter on low heat. Add 1/3 cup brown sugar and 1/3 cup light corn syrup. Bring to boil on high, *stirring.*

Remove pan from heat and add 1/4 cup flour and 1 teaspoon vanilla.

Then add 2-1/2 cups mixed, unsalted nuts of any kind, along with 1 cup shredded coconut (can even add mini-marshmallows if you like)—mix well. Pour into pan, spread evenly. Bake at 325° till golden brown, about thirty minutes. Invert on rack and cool. Carefully peel foil off heart, invert onto different rack so top is up. Cool well. Decorate by writing on top with white frosting. If the baked confection is too soft, put it on a piece of heart-shaped cardboard. You could write: "I'm *Coco-Nuts* for You."

- Make heart-shaped brownies, cookies, biscuits. Check magazines and cookbooks to find ideas for pastries that are sure to gladden someone's heart.
- Cards. Make them yourself. Use satin ribbon, dried flowers, lace. Find verses in books of poetry or from Shakespeare.
- Make a bundle! Take a pretty piece of material, a scarf, or a hanky, fill with kisses and wrap with pretty ribbon. You could say something like "I love you a bundle and a bunch!"
- Don't wait in line at a crowded restaurant and *spend* a bundle. Treat the love of your life to a candlelight picnic on the living room floor. Move some furniture and spread a blanket. Put on soft music. And don't tell her *that* you love her, tell her *why*. You tell him, too!

Easter (Date Changes Each Year):

It is not necessary to give gifts at Easter time, but there are some traditions *and* reasons that present themselves:

- The old standard Easter basket. This is primarily for children, but even teens appreciate an Easter basket. Filled with candy, it was always a welcome sight after weeks of Lenten sacrifice.
- A heavy jar filled with jelly beans.
- An Easter lily.
- An inspirational book that captures the essence of redemption. *Pilgrim's Progress* is a wonderful classic that would fit this bill nicely.
- Blown out and decorated eggs. These can be homemade or purchased.
- A collection of flower bulbs for planting.
- A gourmet or imported ham.

- A live rabbit as a pet for a child. Warning! Don't do this without talking to the child's parents, if you are not the parent. Remember, this is a *live* rabbit.
- A tape of a Gregorian chant.
- The gift of reconciliation. Maybe this would be a good time to write a note or make a phone call to someone from whom you've been separated.

Secretary's Day, End of April

- The day off, with pay.
- Tickets to a special luncheon given just for secretaries.
- Gift certificate to a good clothing store.
- Flowers.
- A pen set for the desk.
- A nicely engraved nameplate.
- A raise.
- A note that expresses your appreciation.
- A designated parking spot.
- *You* make the coffee!

Mother's Day, Second Sunday in May

What to do for Mom? Sure, you can get her a *thing*, maybe even something she wants, but let's consider some other ideas as well:

- This won't work for everyone, but most mothers would be thrilled to have their clan all around them on this special day. Moms like to see everyone together (and getting along). It's a mother thing.

- Take Mom to brunch or dinner. I know it's the busiest day of the year for restaurants, but find a good place, make reservations early, and go.
- Take Mom to tea someplace special, just the two of you. Get all dressed up. Take your time.
- Don't you dare let Mom lift a finger today!
- A mother's ring with birthstones of all her children would be a sweet gift. There are other pieces of jewelry to consider as well.
- Mom in a nursing home or in the hospital? Do what one woman did: haul over your mom's china and a couple of her friends to the house or hospital and host a tea party.
- Present Mom with a photo album or scrapbook that includes pictures, events, awards, and memorabilia of each of her children. It needn't be extensive: just enough to give her "bragging" rights.
- Treat Mom to a complete spa experience: color analysis, makeup consultation, manicure, pedicure, massage, facial: the works! Wrap her in a new terry cloth bathrobe.
- Make a homemade card and tell her *why* you are glad she is your mom.
- Plant a cluster of flower bulbs in a lovely spot on your property, or get permission to do so at a church or a park. Mom's heart will flutter with joy when she passes that spot and knows that those are "her" flowers!
- Don't talk back.

Father's Day, Second Sunday in June

You know what? I think Dad gets short shrift. I really do. I'm not sure we all understand how hard Dad works toward our good:

- Soak his feet and massage those hands that work so hard.
- Clean his car or truck from top to bottom. If you can all pitch in, you might be able to afford to have the vehicle "detailed" by a professional firm.
- Send him to the health club for an hour-long massage. Careful! Ask for the kind that is relaxing, not one of those deep-tissue torture episodes.
- Plant a tree in your father's honor. Make a homemade plaque to hang on a branch. If you don't have space to plant it, get permission from a local church or park. Take an annual picture of "Dad's tree" and use the picture to adorn your homemade card to him.
- Take Dad to breakfast on Father's Day. Give him a crown or a blue ribbon to wear. He won't feel one bit silly, I promise.
- Give him a new barbecue grill or cookout utensils.
- How about a cup with your "mug" emblazoned on the side?
- Make shaving enjoyable for him: get him a new razor, some quality shave cream, a shaving brush, a special "toner" to prepare his beard *before* shaving.
- Clean the garage or his toolshed. Careful! Don't upset his apple cart! Make sure you don't throw anything away, and that he can find things afterwards. A dad's world is sometimes ordered chaos!
- Stick him in a hammock and cut the grass.
- Tell him why you're glad he's your dad.
- Take him fishing.

Grandparents' Day, Second Sunday in September

- Bragging rights! No gram or gramps should leave home without them! Put together a convenient accordion-style photo album with all the little munchkins' (or even big munchkins') pictures inside.
- A letter telling grandparents why they are number one. Josh, for sure, would zero in on Grandma-from-the-Bronx for her sense of humor, and his other grandma for her chocolate-chip cookies.
- A bit of history from the family tree. Hire someone to trace your genealogy.
- A picture of the grandchild/ren in a frame that can be used for subsequent pictures. Many old folks end up with so many pictures they are crowded out of their living room! Use common sense. Give one sturdy frame for each child, and if possible, *you* install each year's new school picture for the person.
- A silver charm for Grandma's bracelet for each new grandchild. Make it gold for the great-grandchildren.
- A "Bubbe" pendent for the Jewish grandma.
- A video of the family at a picnic, reunion, wedding, holiday celebration: nothing would make Gram or Gramps happier than to watch that video of their family over and over.
- A recipe book for Grandma—with a twist. Ask your preschooler to dictate a few recipes to you: how to make a pizza, how to cook a turkey, how to bake a cake. Try not to smudge the recipe cards with your tears of laughter! (Young Austin Soper from New Orleans has pizza down to a science: "You call the deliverman, and when it comes you put it in the oven, and then you wash your hands and eat it.")

Thanksgiving, Last Thursday in November

This holiday presents us with the need for a hostess gift more than any other. It is not traditional to exchange gifts on this day. But what can you *bring* when you visit someone for dinner?

- Pie. Pumpkin, cherry, apple, and pecan pie seem to be the pies of choice for this holiday. Offer to make (or buy) a few. It will relieve some of the burden of meal preparation.
- Bread, rolls, biscuits. Don't worry about duplicating something; these freeze nicely and with the weeks of holiday entertaining ahead, will be welcome. As a matter of fact, consider making sturdy rolls specifically for use in turkey sandwiches.
- Jello dishes. Remember! There's always room for Jello!
- A seasonal and festive tablecloth.
- A big platter or a cake stand.
- Jars of your home-canned fruits, veggies, and jams.
- A selection of gourmet mustards and chutneys.
- A gallon of cider.
- Candles, especially scented pillar candles.
- Scented potpourri.
- A basket of Christmas wrapping supplies.
- A potted bulb that will flower during the Christmas season.
- A tape of Christmas music.
- Dish towels.
- A quality pepper mill and a collection of exotic peppercorns.
- An Advent storybook.*
- An Advent calendar.
- An Advent wreath.

* *Jotham's Journey*, Servant Publications

Chanukah, Early Winter

This is an eight-day Jewish festival with both historic and seasonal origins. It is customary to give a gift on each of the eight days.

- Chanukah *gelt*. This is the custom of giving children money.
- A menorah, which is a candleholder to hold the candles lit on each of the eight days.
- A dreidl. This is a four-sided top with a letter on each side. A popular Chanukah game is played with the dreidl.
- Board games, toys.
- Jelly doughnuts.
- Candles.
- Cloth dreidl filled with wrapped hard candies and candy money.
- The Book of Judith.

Christmas, December 25

If there is one holiday that gives you creative license, it is Christmas. This is a time when "homemade" abounds. As more of us recognize the *reason* for the season, homemade sentimental gifts are highlighted, and reckless spending is stamped with "Bah! Humbug!"

- A crèche.
- A tape or CD of Christmas carols and hymns.
- An evergreen wreath.
- An ice-cream Yule log from a specialty shop.
- Mistletoe and holly.
- A video presentation of the Nativity.
- A handmade or hand-knit Christmas stocking.
- A punch bowl.

- Green and red cloth napkins and table runner.
- Bundles of firewood to use as starter or to scent the fire. Right now, I'm pruning leaves and small branches from bush trimmings to create short sticks, which I will bundle, tie with twine, and present at Christmastime to friends who like a touch of rustic. I may incorporate a pine bough and bells to make a "stick-bundle door ornament."
- Slipper socks.
- Fudge.
- A tree skirt made of felt with each person's name glued on with glitter.
- A Christmas cactus in bloom, or a poinsettia.
- A HUGE bag of mixed nuts and a nutcracker.
- Good cheer—call someone and express it.

Kwanzaa, December 26 to 31

Swahili for "first fruits," this African-American holiday is observed for seven days beginning December 26. It is a celebration of black culture. Here the intent in gift-giving is to present another with something personally made, so the gift then bears your "spirit." The colors green and black are culturally significant.

- Something crafted from wood. Perhaps a picture frame. Extra points if you take a picture of the recipient and put it inside the frame.
- A quilt, or quilted place mats, using green and black as dominant colors.
- An afghan in green and black.
- Something in needlepoint or cross-stitch.
- A piece of jewelry you made. You might purchase beads at a

specialty shop and string them on thin rawhide. You could make bracelets and necklaces this way.

- Something from your kitchen. Make a salad with couscous and peanuts.
- If I were presenting a gift, I would write a poem, or a tribute on pretty parchment paper to go with the gift.
- What could be a greater gift than to extend your hand in true friendship to an African-American, and to work for justice and equality and a world that does not see color?

10

For Kids Only
NO ONE OVER TWELVE ALLOWED!

Dear Parents:

No peeking! This section is the exclusive domain of kids of the twelve-and-under variety. With the help of some young friends, this chapter was created with the skills and financial restrictions of children in mind, and was written with language that kids can understand. If youngsters live in your home, tell them about this chapter—and leave the book in an obvious place (like in the refrigerator!). Children have reasons to give gifts, too, and one of them is probably *you!*

❧

Dear Kids:

I want to be able to help you come up with ideas for gifts for your family and your friends. And I want to help you figure out how to pay for the gifts, too! So I asked my young friends Laura, Taylor, and Cameron, and my nieces, Olivia and Leah, to help me write this chapter just for you. They ate a huge pepperoni pizza while I asked them questions about stuff.

Have you ever thought about why you give someone a gift? Laura and Taylor said it's because you love people and you know a gift will make them feel happy. We feel happy when we get gifts from people we love, don't we? Cameron, who is only six, says we should also think about giving gifts to people who don't have many friends. I like that idea, don't you?

Here's What Olivia Had to Say

Gifts. I always wonder what I'm going to give my friends, sister, relatives, and parents. Sometimes it's been hard to know what to give, but it really isn't, especially with this book. It narrows things down and makes it easy to give an awesome gift.

I have a pretty long list of people. Do you? So, what do I give all of these people? I want to give presents that people will keep, enjoy, and use. That can be difficult, especially for people who seem to have everything.

Do you have the same problem? Don't worry. Sit down with your favorite teddy and your own list. Think of the people on the list. What would they like? Or need? If you can't think of anything in a couple of minutes, ask the person. If someone says he wants hugs and kisses, WRAP A BOXFUL!

So, why are we even going through all this effort to give special gifts? Because it shows people that we care. You have to admit, as kids, we don't often take the time to think of others. Gift-giving shows them that we do.

Here's What Leah Had to Say

Gifts are important because they make people feel special. I like seeing people happy. Gifts say a lot of things, but mostly they say I care. My favorite gift to give is something I made, especially something to do with nature.

The Best Gift of All

Cameron wanted to talk about kids who don't have many friends. He said the best gift we could give is to be their friend. The other kids said that sometimes it's hard to be friends with some people. "So that's why we SHOULD!" said Cameron. Sometimes it makes other kids feel better about themselves if you hang out with them instead of just the cool kids. How can you do this? Olivia and Laura had the same idea: try to find something you both like so you can have something to talk about or to do together. Other kids feel better when someone likes the same things they like.

The Next Best Gift of All

Taylor wanted to talk about kids who don't have much. It's important for us to remember that there are people who have less than we do. Taylor's parents taught him this. Taylor and his brother and sister have a "Ten Things a Week Club." They go through all of their toys and clothes and books and find ten things that they can give to others who don't have so much. Sharing what you have is a great gift! Even if you gave just one can of soup each week to the food bank, you would help someone else. Maybe you can you start a "One Thing a Week Club"!

Make Your List, and Check It Twice

It is a good idea to think about everyone you want to give a gift to, so you can have a plan. If you write down a person's name you can think about what you want to get—or make! There are lots of ideas in this chapter to help you decide. But first write your list. Make a list for Christmas, just for practice. Your list could look like this:

CHRISTMAS		
NAME	GIFT IDEA	BUDGET

Oh Great! So What Do You Do NOW?

Some of you have a pretty long list, don't you? Maybe some of the people will just get a nice homemade card or a bookmark this year! But if you want to do more for Mom, Dad, and Grandma, keep reading.

Free Gifts

We can give some gifts that don't cost any money. They do cost *something*, though, and that is our time and our effort. Give a certificate that has a promise written on it! But remember! A promise is a promise! Here are some rad ideas:

I promise to clean my room before I am old enough to shave.

I promise to clean my room before I leave for college.

This certificate is good for one fifteen-minute hand, back, or foot massage.

Redeem this coupon for a handy-dandy, spotless car cleaning.

This valuable coupon is good for one "Yes" when I really want to say "No."

Kids in the kitchen only! This certificate is good for one kid-made, homemade dinner. (Don't panic, I'll turn off the stove!)

Hop in the hammock, Dad! I'll cut the grass.

Stay in bed, dearest Mother! Breakfast is served! (You tell me when.)

OK, OK. I'll do the dishes.

OK, OK. I'll go to bed on time. (Just this once!)

I promise to feed the dog, the cat, the fish, the horse, the gerbil. This is a one-week guarantee.

I promise to walk the dog. This is a one-month guarantee.

This certificate is good for one complete housecleaning.

I pledge to read one book to you, beginning tonight. You pick the book. (But don't make it too hard!)

I will not watch TV or videos on Wednesdays for one month. I will spend time with you instead.

This coupon is good for forever kisses and hugs. (Just not in front of my friends, please!)

Make It Yourself!

If you want to give something other than a certificate and you don't have any money, you can make it yourself. There are lots of ideas in this book to help you (Yes, it's OK if you read it.) And you can find all kinds of other ideas in craft books at the library. If you don't know how to find a book in the library, ask one of the people who work there. It is their job to help you, and they will be happy to do so.

Even if you make something, you might need *some* money to buy parts. How does a kid come up with money?

1. If you get an allowance, start to put aside some of it each week.

2. If you have permission from your parents, ask your relatives or neighbors for work to do. Maybe your parents have a special job you could do to make a little extra money.

3. If it's a gift for Mom, ask Dad for some help. If it's a gift for Dad, ask Mom. You could also ask a grandparent or older brother or sister for a small loan.

4. Olivia made and sold dog biscuits once. You could have a lemonade stand, sell cookies, collect aluminum cans and sell them to the recycling center.

Stuff to Make for Special Occasions

If you don't think you can do some of this by yourself, ask a grown-up to help!

Christmastime

EAT YOUR SPINACH AND MAKE TIN-CAN LUMINARIES!

You need:

a collection of tin cans, the bigger the better

a big nail

a piece of round wood

a hammer

short candles

Collect tin cans from the garbage and clean them well. Take off the wrappers and labels. Punch holes in the side of the can, using a hammer and nails. You need a piece of round wood to fit the can on so it doesn't bend when you punch your holes. Try to make a nice design. Put small, short candles inside each can. Tell your parents they should line the outside walk to your house with the cans on Christmas night. Light the candles.

Variation: Use the bottom halves of paper milk cartons instead of cans, and punch a design. Place the candle in the center on top of some sand or kitty litter.

THIS IS FOR THE BIRDS

Does someone you know like to watch birds? Roll a pine cone in peanut butter and then roll it in bird seed. Tie string, ribbon, or yarn to the pine cone so it can be attached to an outside branch.

Hey! You could decorate an outside tree for Christmas! It doesn't have to be a pine tree! It could even be a bush! Just pick one that is near a window so everyone inside can see it.

MAKE A GARLAND!

You need:
strong nylon thread or fishing line
a big needle
cranberries, popcorn, or small bells

Put thread in the needle and run the needle through the middle of the cranberries, popcorn, or bells. You could use all three! Make a long garland to wrap around your Christmas tree. Make sure to tie a very big knot at the end so everything doesn't fall off!

DECORATE A LITTLE TREE

What better gift could you give your grandparents or a lonely person in a nursing home than a small Christmas tree decorated with homemade ornaments? Maybe you could make a tiny cranberry garland!

MAKE A WREATH

You need: a wire coat hanger
the kind of wire florists use, or strong string
pine cones
small pine tree branches
red ribbon

Make a circle out of the wire. Use florist wire or string to attach pine tree branches to the circle. Make sure you put enough branches on to make it look full. Attach pine cones all over the wreath with red ribbons.

MAKE AN ORNAMENT

You need:
felt (buy at a fabric or hobby store)
glue
scissors
buttons, ribbons, pine cones, beads, Life Savers candies

glue a ribbon on for a hanger.

glue buttons and ribbons on for decorations

green felt

brown felt

Think of different designs you'd like to cut: angels, Christmas trees, Christmas stockings, round balls, candy canes. Once you cut the designs, use all the other stuff to decorate, using the glue. You could even use different colors of felt to make pretty designs. Remember that the traditional colors for Christmas are red and green.

Do Someone a Favor:

MAKE SMALL GIFTS FOR THE TABLE

You need:

leftover cardboard rolls from toilet paper

aluminum foil

pretty labels

curly ribbon

candy kisses

magic marker

Cut a piece of aluminum foil large enough to cover the cardboard roll. Put candy inside the roll, then roll it up in the foil. You should have two long ends of foil sticking out, one on each side. Pinch the ends of the foil closed on each side. Tie colorful curly ribbon on each pinch. Put a pretty sticker on the side of the tube, and write someone's name with magic marker. This is a terrific gift to put in someone's stocking or on someone's pillow.

NAME THE PLACE

Tell Mom or Dad that you want to make name cards for all of your family or guests for Christmas dinner. Use your imagination—and colorful paper and magic markers! Know what? You could make place cards people can eat! Decorate big Christmas cookies with a person's name, glue the cookie with frosting to another sturdy cookie. Put on top of everyone's plate. Way cool!

MAKE A GRAHAM CRACKER HOUSE

You need:

graham crackers

white frosting

candies for decoration

"Build" graham cracker walls by using thick frosting as glue. Use graham crackers for the roof, too, then frost the roof with the white frosting so it looks like snow. Use frosting and candy to make doors, windows, or decorations.

MAKE A CANDLEHOLDER FOR MOM

You need:

a short, clear, glass jar with a wide opening

glue

foil garland (see if there is some in your Christmas decorations) or pretty ribbon

a colorful button or bell

a short candle

Glue the garland or ribbon around the outside top of the jar, and attach buttons or bells with more glue. Put the candle inside. If you really want to be clever, mix a tiny drop of food coloring into salt or sugar, just enough to cover the bottom of the jar. Put the candle on top of that.

START YOUR OWN TRADITION
WITH POPCORN BALLS

You need:

adult supervision

a huge bowl

popped popcorn

marshmallows

margarine

colorful plastic wrap

ribbon

Turn to page 53 for my easy recipe for popcorn balls. Read about how I give them to friends each year. You could, too! It's a great gift that just about *everybody* likes.

Valentine's Day

Here are several ways to give someone your heart.

MAKE A HEART NECKLACE

You need:

pink, white, and red polymer clay (available at craft stores).

Make 12-inch ropes of each color, then braid together. Shape your braid into a heart and put it on a cookie sheet. Bake at 275° for 15 minutes. Let it cool before you attach to a ribbon to make a necklace.

- Look in a cookbook for an easy sugar cookie recipe. Use a heart-shaped cookie cutter. Make, bake, and tie the cookie cutter to your bundle of cookies as part of the gift.
- Cut out a red heart from paper and put stickers all over it to make a happy Valentine.
- Make a lace heart from paper doilies or use a tack, and punch holes all over the edges of a paper heart you make from white paper. Glue a smaller red heart on top of the lace, write your message on the red heart.
- Cut out a pale pink paper heart, put lipstick on your lips and put kisses all over the card and envelope for a Valentine's Day card.
- Glue candy hearts to a frame that has your picture inside.

Something Special for Dad
- Make a tie out of red construction paper, and glue pink hearts all over it. Use paper clips to attach it to his shirt.

Something Special for Mom
WHITE BREAD FLOWERS

You need:

1 slice of white bread without crust

1 tablespoon Elmers glue

red and green food coloring

toothpicks

Mush together 1/2 Tablespoon of glue, 1/2 the bread, and a tiny drop of red food coloring until it feels like play dough. (This could take thirty minutes or an hour, so you'll have to help, Mom and Dad.)

Mush the other half of the ingredients with a tiny drop of green coloring.

Next, take a piece of dough about the size of the end of your thumb, roll into a spiral and put on a toothpick for the center of your flower.

Make petals with the bread by rolling a tiny ball and then smashing it between thumb and index finger.

Stick these all around the flower center.

Then attach green leaves.

Let your flowers dry a few days.

Something Special for Dad or Mom

Make a trail with chocolate candy kisses. Write little messages of love along the trail. Trails could lead to: Mom's pillow, the refrigerator, the mailbox, her dinner plate or the phone. Surprise her with a small heart-shaped box of chocolates at the end of the trail.

You could do this for Dad, too. Make a trail that leads to his: tie rack, night stand, car seat, shower, or briefcase.

Special Breakfast for Mom and Dad

Serve French toast or pancakes that are shaped like hearts. Put strawberries on the plate. Yum!

Something Very Special

Fill a tin with notes of love. Tell Mom or Dad to take one out each night and read it before going to bed.

Mother's Day

Kids, if there is *one* holiday you don't want to forget, this is it! Think of everything your mother does for you. Think how hard she works. This is a good time to show her how much she means to you. Mothers *really* like things that you make yourself. Here are some ideas:

- Hankie Potpourri. Ask Grandma or one of your aunts for an old lace hankie. Go for a walk and look for buds of flowers that smell pretty. Pick some, but *not* from a neighbor's yard. Wild rosebuds are awesome for this. Try to let the buds dry out for a few days. If they lose their smell, spray some pretty perfume on them. Then wrap them all in a hankie like a bundle. Tie the bundle with a pretty ribbon.
- Glue dried wildflowers or small pinecones to a wooden picture frame that has your school picture in it.
- Pick field flowers and make a pretty bouquet for Mom. If you live in a city and there is a flower shop nearby, stop by and ask them if you can sweep the sidewalk in exchange for

some flowers. Some florists throw older flowers away. If you find some near the shop, ask politely if you may have them.

- Don't let Mom lift a finger on her day. Set the dinner table for a queen. Make dinner very, very special on Mother's Day. Use a tablecloth and cook dinner yourself!

- Draw Mom a picture of her favorite spot or of her doing something she really likes to do. When my son was young, he drew a picture of me playing the piano. I still have that picture.

- Put on a performance: write a play and perform it with your brothers and sisters—or all by yourself! Sing a song, dance, put on a puppet show. Make Mom laugh!

- Write your mother a letter. Don't just tell her you love her, tell her *why* you love her. What makes her so special to you? If it is the way she smiles, the way she holds you, the way she makes you feel safe and protected, or the way she cooks, tell her. You could turn your letter into a small booklet and draw pictures of how you feel.

- Find a fat blue ribbon and write "#1 Mom" on it.

- Give her a box filled with imaginary kisses and hugs.

- Make her take a nap. Read to her while she falls asleep. Give her a kiss on the cheek.

- Ask someone to take you shopping and buy some flower bulbs. Find a spot in your yard where you can plant the bulbs and create "Mom's Pretty Garden." If you don't have a yard, ask a friend if you can make a special garden for your mother in his yard, or ask your church if you can plant the bulbs on church property. Every single year when the flowers bloom, your mom will be so happy to know that it is her very own special spot, planted just by you!

Three Great Ideas!

1. This is what Taylor did for his mom one year: He made a card that looked like a flowerpot, with a small paper pocket glued on the front. He traced his hand on construction paper and used the outline of his hand as "flowers" that he slipped inside the pocket. Each hand-flower had a different message: take out trash, give hugs and kisses, do dishes, make bed, make breakfast, do laundry.

2. Laura gave her mother bath salts she made.
   You need:
   3 cups of Epsom salts (buy at drugstore)
   1 Tablespoon of glycerin
   2 drops of food coloring
   perfume

   Put the salts in a glass or metal container. In a separate bowl combine glycerin and food coloring. Then add four drops of perfume. Add this mixture to the Epsom salts. Stir thoroughly.

3. One year, Taylor made a "Mother's Day Cookbook" for his mom. He punched holes in all of his recipe cards and tied the cards together with red yarn. He even had a table of contents. Taylor collected some recipes from friends. His mom's favorite was "Nibble Nests." Here it is:
   You need:
   7 ounces of marshmallow creme
   1/2 cup peanut butter
   4 Tablespoons of soft margarine
   8-1/2 ounce can of chow mein noodles
   1 bag of jelly bean "eggs"

Mix marshmallow creme, peanut butter, and margarine until blended. Add noodles and mix well. Drop medium spoonfuls into muffin liners. Shape into nests with greased fingers. Let stand until firm. Fill with jelly beans. These would be fun to make at Easter!

An Extra Special Idea!

Decorate Mom's room! Put your homemade card on her pillow, cut out hearts with messages and put them all over her bedroom, use crepe paper and balloons, pick as many wildflowers as you can. Try to make the room shout, "Mom, I love you!"

Father's Day

Don't forget Dad! This is his day, so make it special. What can you do?

- Take Dad fishing or to a ball game. Even better, play ball *with* him. Maybe you can organize a baseball game of your own.
- Ask Mom to help you buy and plant a tree in your dad's honor. Make a homemade sign to hang on the tree. Tell Dad he's the tree trunk and you are a strong branch because of him.
- Write and frame "I LOVE YOU, DAD!"
- Draw a picture of Dad at work.
- Show up at his work with a picnic lunch. Or bring him a plate of chocolate-chip cookies at work and tie a helium balloon to his car.
- Find a photo shop that will put your picture on the side of a

mug. Fill it with coffee and bring it to him while he's shaving.

- Put a special love note in his briefcase, in his lunch pail, or on the steering wheel. If he farms, or has a pet, attach your note with ribbons to one of his favorite animals.
- Make him King-for-a-Day. Make a crown and use his bathrobe as a robe. Soak his feet and give him a foot massage.
- Make a bookmark that says "I love you, Dad!" Maybe you can find a feather or pretty flower to glue on the bookmark. Take it to a copy shop and ask them to laminate it.
- Mow the lawn.
- Clean the garage.
- Make a campfire. Sit around your fire at night and roast marshmallows. Ask Dad to tell you what it was like when he was your age.

Grandparents' Day

- Make a soap dish out of a big seashell. Find a pretty bar of soap to put inside.
- Write a funny story about your family, then read it to Grandma.
- Write a poem about why your grandparents are special to you.
- Go for a hike and find the perfect walking stick for Gramps. Hang leather shoelaces and feathers from the top. If he lives in bear country, attach a bell.
- Ask an adult to take a videotape of you doing something that would please your grandparents. Can you play an

instrument? Can you read well? Can you sing? Can you jump really high? Can you run fast?

- Go to your grandparents' house and make tea and cookies. Then have a tea party.
- Help your grandparents in any way you can: cut the grass, clean the car, clean the oven. Older people sometimes need help with these things.
- Make a big star out of construction paper and paste your school picture in the middle. Tell your grandparents that you are a part of their constellation!
- Make a special family photo album. Did you all get together at the lake last year? Were you all together for Thanksgiving dinner? Did you all go to a wedding? Make a photo album just of that. Write funny sentences under the pictures.

HOMEMADE HEATING PAD

You may need the help of an adult with a sewing machine for this one.

You need:

rice

flannel cloth

Sew the flannel cloth in a rectangle, about a foot long and eight inches wide. Fill with rice. Make sure the bag is sewn tightly so the rice can't fall out. Tell your grandpa to heat this in the oven at 275° for ten minutes. This is a wonderful heating pad.

For a Friend's Birthday

Mom usually helps you and buys the gift for you to bring to a party, but what if this is a special friend and you want to give a present you thought of yourself?

For Girls

- Does she have a Barbie or a favorite doll? Maybe you can make or buy doll clothes.
- Paper dolls are always fun.
- Most young girls like horse or dog books.
- A stuffed animal is a sure hit.
- Would your friend like dollhouse furniture? Maybe you can create some miniatures all by yourself. Olivia has a small barn for her play horses. Her friend made tiny straw bales and oat bags. She even made watering cans out of film canisters!
- If your friend has a dog, braid three long sections of leftover fabric that are about one-inch wide. This makes a neat dog collar. Tie it loosely around the dog's neck.
- Stamps, stamp pads, and stickers are fun presents.
- Make a friendship bracelet.
- Get some T-shirt paint and design a one-of-kind T-shirt for your one-of-a-kind friend.
- Decorate a straw hat. Get crazy. Hang lollipops off the brim.
- String beads and make a necklace. Give beads to older kids as a gift.
- Does your friend share her deepest secrets with you? Buy her a diary.

MAKE FACE PAINTS

And then make faces! Use a muffin tin to mix colors separately.

For each color, you need:

1 teaspoon cornstarch

1/2 teaspoon cold cream

1/2 teaspoon water

food coloring (add one drop at a time)

Great Idea If She Loves Her Pet

Get a picture of your friend's favorite pet and bring it to a copy shop. Ask the clerk how much it would cost to make the picture into a poster. Wouldn't she just love to hang it in her room?

For Boys

- Make a kite. Crisscross a couple of dowels, tie them together with wire. Use a white trash sack as the kite material, decorate with magic markers.
- Does your friend live in the city? Get him some sidewalk chalk.
- Cameron came up with this idea: take an empty tissue box and put rubber bands over the opening. Instant banjo!
- Bet your buddy would like a rad squirt gun—or some water balloons. Just don't get into trouble! Watch who you get wet.
- Check with his parents first, and if they say OK, you might get a pocketknife for your friend.
- Does he fish? Buy him some hooks and lures. Can't have enough, you know.

- Every single boy on the planet collects baseball cards.
- Get Mom to help you paint plastic toy soldiers with her nail polish. Or paint a plain, white plastic toy, like an airplane.
- A water bottle for a bike is cool. This is good for a boy *or* a girl.
- Does your friend read sports books or detective stories? Buy him one.
- Decorate a baseball cap, or buy a cap of a favorite pro team.
- There is so much a fellow can do with a tennis ball. Give him one.
- School time? Give him some pencils with fat erasers.

Something You Can Do

Give your friend play clay that you made yourself.

PLAY CLAY

You need:
one cup of plain flour
1/2 cup salt
one Tablespoon oil
1 teaspoon cream of tartar
3/4 cup water
food coloring

Mix ingredients together in a large bowl.

For a Grown-Up's Birthday

- Use acrylic paint (you find it in the craft section of big stores) to decorate a bottle or a glass or flowerpot.
- If the person likes to garden, do what I did. I made plant markers out of paint stirrers. Go to a paint store and ask for the wooden "sticks" they give to mix paint. Cut them in half. Use a fat magic marker to write the name of the plant across them, such as SPINACH (yuck!), TOMATO, EGGPLANT (double yuck!). Get some thick string or twine and tie the markers to foot-long sticks, making it look sort of like a cross.

- Get some clay and make a molded candleholder. You could use cookie cutters to make a shape.
- Wrap an empty tin can with wrapping paper or aluminum foil. Decorate with stickers or ribbon. Stick some pencils inside.

- Write your birthday wishes on a piece of birch bark.
- Make a necklace out of macaroni shells or buttons. Or go to a craft store and buy a bunch of inexpensive charms. String them together with safety pins or fishing swivels (ask Dad for these).
- Make pretty stationery. Use stamps, colorful pens, stencils, or stickers to decorate plain white paper.
- Record your birthday message on a tape. It will become a special treasure.
- Make your own checkers. Glue squares of black and red construction paper to cardboard. Use buttons as checkers.
- Make a "baseball card" of *you!* If you need help, stop by a copy shop and tell them what you have in mind.
- Do what Olivia does—make a mix. Olivia puts all the dry ingredients for a cookie recipe in a jar and presents it with a recipe. She decorates the jar of mix with ribbon.
- Do what Leah does—make tea. Leah combines her own concoction of thyme, orange peel, lemon grass, and rosebuds to make her own tea. It's good! Ask an adult to help you invent a tea too!

An Awesome Gift Idea

You need an adult to help you *just a little* with this project, but it is worth it! Go for a hike in the woods or on a beach. Collect as many short, stubby pieces of wood as you can find. They should all be at least six inches, but no more than a foot long. Get a long piece of sturdy wire. Drill a hole in the middle of each piece of wood, and "string" the wood pieces on the wire. You will have to tie the wire on the bottom so the wood doesn't fall off. Make this mobile as long as you like. My young friends and I make them about four feet long. They should be hung outside, alongside someone's house or cabin.

A "Chiming" Idea

Visit a thrift store and buy old silverware. Ask an adult to drill a hole in the top of each piece. Hang the knives, spoons, and forks from a piece of wood to create a wind chime.

11

Particular Presents for Particular People
FROM A TO Z,
A SIMPLE-TO-FOLLOW
WISH LIST

Is Grandpa a fisherman? Does Uncle Bill belong to a volunteer fire department? Does Cousin Irene putter in her garden? Is Aunt Mary a dentist? How about getting a gift that fits someone's occupation or interest? Read on for suggestions from A to Z. Gift suggestions include everything from very low-cost (i.e. homemade) to the more pricey (i.e. group gift). Most categories are followed by a catalogue and magazine address. The catalogue is for advance planning. For instance, if you want to surprise Uncle Bill with "FD" cufflinks, you will find them in the "fireman" catalogue. You might also ask to have the catalogue sent to him. Please consider two things: catalogue buying is often more pricey, and merchants in your town might have the same product—with local service!

Each category lists a magazine. A gift subscription is just one suggestion for a gift. For instance, Irene, who putters in the garden, might be thrilled to get *Organic Gardening* every other month.

Note: Many professionals may already receive the magazine recommended. It is wise to check with a secretary or office manager to make certain you are not duplicating a subscription.

Accountant: a good mechanical pencil, pen and pencil set, desk organizer, desk pad or blotter, pencil sharpener, whimsical figurine of accountant, small portable calculator

Catalogue: *Reliable Office Supplies*, (800) 735-4000

Magazine: *Accounting Technology*, 11 Penn Plaza, New York, New York 10001, (800) 535-8403.

Architect: drawing tubes for airline carry-on, fine-line drawing pencils, stylist pens, humorous style drafting templates, scale plan wheel, rapiograph pen and ink set, specific topic reference books, drafting-desk organizer, prisma color pen set

Catalogue: *Dataprint*, (800) 227-6191

Magazine: *Architectural Digest*, 6300 Wilshire Blvd. Suite 1100, Los Angeles, CA 90048, (213) 965-3700.

Attorney: paperweight, gavel, nameplate for door or desk, red tie, manicure set, letter opener, leather briefcase or leather folder for papers

Catalogue: *Lawyer's Stationery*, (800) 252-1826

Magazine: *Student Lawyer*, 750 N. Lake Shore Drive, Chicago, IL 60611, (312) 988-6048.

Baker: digital timers, parchment paper, baking pans, specialty cookbook (such as for breads, scones, pastries), marble slab and rolling pin, expensive vanilla, cake-decorating supplies, measuring cups and spoons, cooling racks, apron

> Catalogue: *Williams-Sonoma,* (800) 541-1262
>
> Magazine: *Fine Cooking,* P.O. Box 5506, Newton, CT 06470, (203) 426-8171.

Bicyclist: pack for under seat, tool kit, patch kit, water bottle, tire sealer, helmet, gloves, Leatherman tool, pump, tights, jerseys, flat-fixing kit

> Catalogue: *Bike Nash Bar,* (800) 627-4227
>
> Magazine: *Bicycling,* 33 E. Minor Street, Emmaus, PA 18098. (610) 967-5171

Boating Enthusiast: sunscreen, nautical theme towels or napkins, life preservers, picnic cooler, boater's hat, ropes for boat, thermos, barometer, bright flashlight, compass

> Catalogue: *West Marine Products,* (800) 538-0075
>
> Magazine: *Motor Boat & Sailing,* 250 W 55th St., New York, NY 10019, (212) 649-4099.

Camping or Outdoor Enthusiast: package of moleskin, fanny pack, sturdy pencil wrapped with duct tape (tape or pencil when needed), bandanna, thermometer, weatherproof matches, birch bark or pitchwood for fire-starting, homemade first aid kit in metal Band-Aid box or sack, utensil set, freeze-dried food packets, nylon rain gear, bungie cords, "croakies" (eyeglass holders), Leatherman tool, binoculars, flashlight, compass

Catalogue: *REI,* (800) 426-4840

Magazine: *Campers Monthly,* P.O. Box 260, Quakertown, PA 18951, (215) 536-6420.

Canoeists: hat, sunscreen that doesn't wash off, dry bag, life preserver, river guide books, water shoes, neoprene socks, yoke carrier for portage

Catalogue: *L.L. Bean,* (800) 341-4341

Magazine: *Canoe & Kayak Magazine,* P.O. Box 3146, Kirkland, WA 98083, (206) 827-6363.

Car Buff: chamois skins, manuals for specific cars, leather steering wheel cover, windshield compass, visor organizer, car freshener, floor mats, key chain with emblem of car model, chrome license-plate cover

Catalogue: *Griot's,* (206) 922-2400

Magazine: *Car & Driver,* 2002 Hogback Road, Ann Arbor, MI 48105-9736, (313) 971-3600.

Carpenter: leather tool belt, carpenter pencils, nail apron, tool chests or organizers of every size, leather gloves, cordless power tools, insulated lunch pail, rain gear, "torpedo" level

Catalogue: *Trend Lines,* (800) 877-7899

Magazine: *Remodeling,* One Thomas Circle NW, Suite 600 Washington, DC 20005, (202) 452-0800.

Cat Lover: note cards with pictures of cats, cat toys, clothes brush with sponge to remove cat hair, costume jewelry with cats, catnip, scratching block, cat carrier

Catalogue: *Cats, Cats, & More Cats*, (914) 782-4141

Magazine: *Cats Magazine,* P.O. Box 290037, Port Orange, FL 32129-0037, (904) 788-2770.

Chiropractor: if you cross-stitch, emblazon a sweatshirt with "Body by God, Fine Tuning By _____" (fill in the name of your chiropractor), words of appreciation, plates of cookies for office staff, an anatomical part, such as a vertebra from an animal, desk set

Catalogue: Palmer College of Chiropractic, (800) 722-2586

Magazine: *American Chiropractic Assoc. Magazine,* 1701 Clarendon Blvd., Arlington, VA 22209, (800) 368-3083 (ask for bookstore catalogue).

Computer Whiz: box of disks, software, wrist rest, pull-out keyboard drawer, mouse pad, anti-glare screen, dust covers for equipment, surge suppresser

Catalogue: *Computer Discount Warehouse,* (800) 3364CDW

Magazine: *PC World,* 501 2nd Street, San Francisco, CA 94107, (415) 243-0500.

Cook: dish towels, hot pads or trivets, whisk, exotic herbs and spices (and instructions on how to *use* them), ethnic cooking class, expensive olive oil, kitchen gadgets, old bowls, recipe card holder (indispensable!), apron

Catalogue: *Colonial Garden Kitchens, (800) 245-3399*

Magazine: *Eating Well,* P.O. Box 54263, Boulder, CO 80323, (800) 678-0541.

Dancer: barrettes, hair net, foot lotion, soothing muscle lotion, sewing kit, music (according to type of dance person does), leotards, dance wear, leg warmers

Catalogue: *Dance Distributors,* (800) 33-DANCE

Magazine: Dance *Magazine,* 33 60th Street, New York, NY 10023, (212) 245-9050.

Dentist/Doctor: nice book for personal use or for waiting room, tickets to a concert, golf items, a quality pen (look for the kind that writes upside down), hand lotion, elk's tooth key chain (for dentist), wood-carved "Doctor" or "Dentist" sign, antique dental equipment

Magazine: *Stitches, The Journal of Medical Humour,* 16787 Warden Avenue, R.R. #3, Newmarket, Ontario L3Y4W1 Canada

Dog Lover: leash (regular or retractable), dog bed, dog toys, offer to "baby-sit" for day/weekend, certificate for dog grooming, biscuits, name tags, dog training video or book, rawhide bone, dog collar, paper towels

Catalogue: *Dogonit Gallery,* (800) 451-3647

Magazine: *Dog Fancy,* P.O. Box 6050, Mission Viejo, CA 92690-6050, (714) 855-8822.

Farmer/Rancher: leather gloves, rain protector for hat, hand salve, bandannas, wool shirt, wool-blend socks, suspenders, battery-operated weather radio, flashlight, sheepskin seat cover for car or tractor, belt buckle

Magazine: *Farm Journal,* W. Washington Square, Dept.
   WM, Philadelphia, PA 19106, (215) 829-4700.

Firefighter: red suspenders, Dalmatian (real thing, or knickknacks) book on old fire engines, belt buckle with fire emblem,
coffee mug, "FD" jewelry or tie, shock-resistant, waterproof
watch
   Catalogue: *Galls, Inc.,* (800) 477-7766
   Magazine: *Firehouse Magazine,* 445 Broad Hollow Road
      Suite 21, Melville, NY 11747, (516) 845-2700.

Fisherman: hand-tied flies, lures, creel, bug spray, guidebooks
on fishing areas, wading boots, rain gear, fish fillet knife, fillet
board, hand-made graphite fly rod ($$)
   Catalogue: *Cabello's ,* (800) 237-4444
   Magazine: *North American Fisherman,* 12301 Whitewater
      Drive, Suite 260, Minnetonka, MN 55343,
      (612) 936-0555.

Gardener: gloves, gardening shears, new variety plant, painters
tray to carry tools in, wooden dowels in variety of sizes, trellis
(exotic or homemade), garden journal, clay pots, crop markers,
antique seeds, seed starter kits, a crying towel
   Catalogue: *Gardener's Eden,* (800) 822-1214
   Magazine: *Organic Gardening,* 33 E. Minor, Emmaus, PA
      18098, (610) 967-5171.

Golfer: balls, tees, gloves, ball retriever, club covers, putter, towel with loop to attach to bag, club brushes, rain umbrella, golf ball retriever (for that water shot!), rain hood for golf bag, rain hat for golfer

    Catalogue: *Edwin Watts Golf Shop,* (800) 874-0146

    Magazine: *Golf Magazine,* 2 Park Avenue, New York, NY
       10016-5695, (212) 779-5000.

Hairdresser/Barber: attractive or humorous calendar, cape, gift certificate at beauty supply store, cork board, business card holder, posters, coffee cup, thick rubber floor mat to cushion feet while standing, holder for blow-dryer and curling irons, shelves

    Magazine: *Modern Salon,* P.O. Box 1414, Lincolnshire, IL
       60069-9912, (847)-634-2600.

Horse Lover: fancy halter or lead rope, saddle blanket, grooming tools, video or book on horse care, advanced riding lessons, saddlebags, horse treats, framed picture of favorite horse

    Catalogue: *Horseman's General Store ,* (800) 343-0167

    Magazine: *Horse Illustrated,* P.O. Box 6050, Mission Viejo,
       CA 92690-8822. (714) 855-3045

Hunter: small leather pouch to carry extra bullets, roll of highway flagging tape for marking locations, gun cleaning solvent and patches, length of flat climbing rope (best rope for pulling game), sharpening stone, hunting videos, gun carrying case, sport shooting vest, Leatherman tool, flare, orange vest

Catalogue: *Cabello's*, (800) 237-4444

Magazine: *Field & Stream*, 2 Park Avenue, New York, NY
10016, (202) 779-5000.

Logger: leather gloves, cold-weather clothes, thermos, insulated lunch pail, steel-toed shoes, sheepskin cover for truck seat,
warm hat, belt buckle

Magazine: *Northern Logger and Timber Processor*, P.O. Box
69, Old Forge, NY 13420, (315) 369-3078.

Mechanic: hand cleaner, tool organizer, shop clothes or cover-
alls, gift certificate for tools, words of appreciation (my mechanic says these are hard to come by)

Magazine: *Popular Mechanics*, 224 W 57th Street, 3rd Floor
New York, NY 10019, (212) 649-2000.

Minister: words of encouragement, small plaques or framed
cross-stitch for the office, books or magazines about current
events or important social issues, gift certificate for dinner out, a
tie, a big bowl of jelly beans.

Catalogue: please check with your local Christian bookstore
or religious supply shop

Magazine: *Leadership*, 465 Gunderson Drive, Carol Stream,
IL 60188, (708) 260-6200.

Model Train Enthusiast: antique pieces, model train cars,
scenery for villages or backdrops, RR paraphernalia, miniature
people or animals, soundtrack of train sounds, switches, engi-
neer's cap

Catalogue: *Terminal Hobby Shop,* (800) 487-2467
Magazine: *Classic Toy Trains,* 21027 Crossroads Circle,
   Waukesha, WI 53187, (414) 796-8776.

Mother-to-Be: maternity clothes, baby books, baby name
book, journal, help at home, pregnancy sling, body lotion, soft
music, long body pillow, reading pillow
   Catalogue: *Motherwear,* (800) 633-0303
   Magazine: *Baby Talk,* P.O. Box 59591, Boulder, CO
      80322, (415) 546-7575.

Motorcycle Enthusiast: leather gloves, tank bag (motorcycle
luggage), one-time disposable camera, mini-mag flashlight,
folding compass, rain suit, ball cap with motorcycle insignia,
sunglasses
   Catalogue: *Chaparral Cycle Supply,* (800) 841-2960
   Magazine: *Rider,* 3601 Calle Tecate, Camarillo, CA
      93012-5040, (805) 389-0300.

Musician: sheet music, music tapes or CDs, carrying case for
small instrument, timer, book of poetry, blank sheets with staffs
for writing music, music stand, certificate for lessons, tickets to a
concert, bow tie
   Catalogue: *Victor Litz Music Center,* (800) 828-5518
   Magazine: *Stereo Review,* 1633 Broadway, New York, NY
      10019, (212) 767-6000.

Nature Lover: walking stick, books on butterflies, mushrooms, birds, trees, or wildflowers, binoculars, small backpack, woolen socks, a compass, leather-bound notebook, magnifying glass, mosquito repellent

Catalogue: *L.L. Bean, (*800) 341-4341

Magazine: *Natural History,* Central Park W at 79th Street, New York, NY 10024, (212) 769-5500.

Nurse: pen that hangs around neck, pen light, festive holiday pins, foot care products, support hose, watch with second hand, hand lotion, "scope coat"—protective cloth cover for stethoscope

Magazine: *Journal of Nursing Jocularity,* P.O. Box 40416, Mesa, AZ 85274, (602) 835-6165.

Old Car/Classic Car Buff: tools to match year of car, period clothing, caps, jewelry with car insignia, anything with car insignia, good liquid or paste wax, magnetic "feather" duster, chamois skins, tire gauge

Catalogue: S*nyder's Antique Auto Part,* (303) 549-5313

Magazine: *Classic Auto Restorer*, P.O. Box 6050, Mission Viejo, CA 92690-6050, (714) 855-8822.

Photographer: frames of various sizes, photo albums, coupons for film processing or enlargements, copies of old family pictures, film, lenses, camera straps, cases for lenses, tripod, slide viewer

Catalogue: *Focus Camera,* (800) 221-0828

Magazine: *Shutterbug Magazine,* 5211 S. Washington Ave., Titusville, FL 32780. (407) 268-5010

Police Officer: expression of thanks, warm gloves, pen that will write in extreme weather conditions, a box of brownies, spill-proof travel mug, alarm clock, a pat on the back

Catalogue: *Tuxall Uniform & Equipment, Inc.,*
(800) 825-3339.

Magazine: *Police Times,* 3801 Biscayne Blvd., Miami, FL 33137. (305) 573-0070

Real Estate Agent: hand-held tape recorder, clipboard, compass with declination, county maps, nice pen, business card holder, daily planner, desk set

Catalogue: *Reliable Home Office,* (800) 326-6230

Magazine: *Journal of Property Management,* P.O. Box 109025, Chicago, IL 60610-9025, (312) 329-6058.

Recreational Vehicle Owner: folding rake, tablecloth clamps, heavy-duty plastic tablecloth, folding table with chairs, tire gauge, indoor/outdoor thermometer, compass, logbook

Catalogue: *National Traveler's RV Center,* (800) 221-4941

Magazine: *RV Times Magazine,* 1100 Welborne Drive Suite 204, Richmond, VA 23229, (804) 741-5376.

Runner/Walker: water bottle, heart-rate monitor, headband, waterproof sunscreen, lightweight vest with reflector, running shorts and tops, tights, Thorlo socks, safety light headgear, shoelaces, pedometer

Catalogue: *Road Runner Sports,* (800) 662-8896

Magazine: *Runner's World,* 33 E. Minor St., Emmaus, PA 18098, (215) 967-5171.

Seamstress/Quilter: stitch ripper, scissors, measuring tapes, patterns, material, how-to books, sewing kit or case, ribbons, buttons, lace, quilting lessons

> Magazine: *Quilting Today Magazine* , 2 Public Ave., Montrose, PA 18801. (717) 278-1984

> Magazine: *Sew News,* P.O. Box 1790, Peoria, IL 61656, (800) .289-6397.

Skier: goggles, gloves, thermal underwear, after-ski slippers, certificate for private lessons, sunglasses, heavy-duty sunscreen and lip and nose protector, gift certificate for tune-up or waxing

> Catalogue: *REI,* (800) 426-4840

> Magazine: *Snow Country,* 5520 Park Ave., Trumbull, CT 06611,. (203) 323-7038

Social Worker: day planner, massage, CD of soft music, telephone answering machine, watch, battery-operated timer, candy, thermos, insulated lunch kit, tank of gas, herbal tea

> Magazine: *Arts & Activities,* 591 Camino de la Reina, Suite 200, Dept WM, San Diego, CA 92108-3104, (619) 297-5353.

Teacher: name plate, candy, flowers, certificate to clothing store, briefcase, red pencil, flower vase, coffee mug, perfume or cologne, tie, holiday jewelry, big red apple

> Catalogue: *Teacher's Pet School Supplies,* (800) 228-2538

> Magazine: *Learning,* 1607 Battleground Ave., Greensboro, NC 27408, (910) 272-8020.

Tennis Player: tickets to local exhibition match, private lessons, balls, racquet, certificate for racquet stringing, sweatbands, socks, sun visor, sunscreen

Catalogue: *Georgia's Tennis,* (800) 821-8211

Magazine: *Tennis Week,* 341 Madison Avenue, New York, NY 10017, (212) 808-4750.

Truck Driver: sun visor organizer for papers, sunglasses, etc., spill-proof mug or water cup, thermos, cushion to aid spinal alignment, tapes or CDs, a "Hurry Home—Safely" note to pin to the dash, your prayers

Magazine: *Inbound Logistics,* 5 Penn Plaza, 8th Floor, New York, NY 10001, (212) 629-1560.

Veterinarian: thank-you cards with picture of pet, books about domestic pets to keep in waiting room, cookie jar for dog "snacks," personalized picture or graphic to hang in office, animal jewelry, treats for the staff, hand cream, good gloves

Magazine: *Cat Fancy* or *Dog Fancy* Box 6050 Mission Viejo, CA 92690, (714) 855-8822.

Zoologist: compass, knife, sunscreen, binoculars, telescope, animal books, zoom lens for camera, pocket tape recorder, sun hat

Catalogue: *L.L. Bean,* (800) 341-4341

Magazine: *Wildlife Conservation Magazine,* 185th Street & Southern Blvd., Bronx, NY 10460-1068, (212) 220-5121.

Appendix

Birthstones

MONTH	STONE	SYMBOLIZES
January	garnet	constancy
February	amethyst	sincerity
March	bloodstone or aquamarine	courage
April	diamond	innocence
May	emerald	love, success
June	pearl or moonstone	health, longevity
July	ruby	contentment
August	sardonyx or peridot	married happiness
September	sapphire	clear thinking
October	opal or tourmaline	hope
November	topaz	fidelity
December	turquoise or lapis lazuli	prosperity

Wedding Anniversary Gift Suggestions

1st	clocks
2nd	china
3rd	crystal and silver
4th	electrical appliances
5th	silverware
6th	wood
7th	desk sets, pens, pencils
8th	linens and laces
9th	leather
10th	diamond jewelry
11th	fashion jewelry
12th	pearls or colored gems
13th	textiles and furs
14th	gold jewelry
15th	watches
16th	hollowware
17th	furniture
18th	porcelain
19th	bronze, figurines
20th	platinum
25th	sterling silver

30th	diamond
35th	jade
40th	ruby
45th	sapphire
50th	golden
55th	emerald
60th	diamond

Flowers

bleeding heart: hopeless, but not heartless

gardenia: I love you in secret

gladiola: you pierce my heart

lily of the valley: let us make up, wedding

rose: I love you passionately

sweet William: you are gallant, suave, perfect

violet: I return your love, happiness

green leaves: hope in a love affair

pansies: thought

rosemary: remembrance

orange blossom: good luck

snowdrops: hope

Index